THE MUGGING OF
KIEL OPERA HOUSE

CIVIC REGRESS

Ed Golterman

ED GOLTERMAN

THE MUGGING OF
KIEL OPERA HOUSE
CIVIC REGRESS

ISBN: 978-0-9815444-0-3
Editor: Alessandra Lopez, Xlibris
Cover and Interior design: Toolbox Creative, www.ToolboxCreative.com
Cover image: Hugh Ferriss (1889–1962)
Interior images: Ed Golterman

Demise or Reopening
Book Two-2010

Photos taken December 31, 2007

TABLE OF CONTENTS

FOREWORD

July 22, 1998

Urban Land Institute Study

Report–Kiel Opera House

Kennedy Room–City Hall

Saint Louis, Missouri

The reporter is capable, experienced, quick, and not new to the market. Her lead question stopped me cold, dropped my heart to my shoes: *Was there really someone named Henry Kiel?*

How can we shape our future if we don't know our past? Had time erased Henry's contributions to St. Louis and placed his remaining *gift* in peril? Had time and her enemies finally *taken* Kiel Opera House, though it stands majestically on Market Street between 14th and 15th?

Henry Kiel was St. Louis' first three-term mayor (1913–1925). Before and after serving as mayor, Kiel Boaz Construction Company built the Missouri, Del Monte, Lowe's State and Ambassador theaters, Kiel Opera House and Convention Hall, Homer G. Phillips Hospital, and children's and community services buildings.

All are gone except Kiel Opera House, which hangs on amid unending attacks by the owners of the Fox Theater and their collaborators. While other cities restore and re-open downtown theaters and concert halls and/or build and open new ones, St. Louis closed, damaged, and wasted the best.

Had we failed to communicate that a *Kennedy Center* downtown, operating year-round, could generate $60 million a year in economic activity on property, four or five times that off property, and deliver substantial tax revenue to a city in need of tax revenue?

Kiel Opera House was closed in 1991 to re-open along with the new hockey arena in 1994 or 1995. In 1995, the puck was dropped on the *back side* of the block. The ball was dropped on the *front side*.

The Opera House has survived damage, exposure to the elements and *gut it for re-use* plots. Millions were spent on *studies* to *soften* the public for the final blow. Reasonable marketing/business plans are ignored by changing ownerships of a hockey team, who control it by lease, and by the City.

Kiel Opera House is the victim but St. Louis suffers. Tourism and business development officials leave because they cannot promote a city without major downtown music arts and culture. Hotel/motel occupancy is too low. The same law firm represents all the *parties* collaborating to *do in* the Opera House. Law is not the only profession diminished by dishonorable work.

Take this journey especially if you have sports-driven deals *coming down* in your city. Take this journey if you have ever battled to save the past to improve the future.

Take this journey if either or both could be on your *horizon*.

There was a Henry Kiel. His great *outdoor* legacy—the Municipal Theater in Forest Park, has been trimmed down to a *token* seven weeks a summer. His great *indoor* legacy, Kiel Opera House, has been wasted 17 years and remains under attack.

About The Author

Ed Golterman was a writer-producer of marketing and training programs, and *book* shows for business theater. Mr. Golterman spent ten years in radio and TV news and sports. He is a concert and show baritone and a life-long student of musical theater. His father, Edward N. Golterman, was an assistant to four St. Louis mayors (Darst, Tucker, Poelker, and Cervantes). His mother, Maria Marceno Golterman, was an operatic soprano.

Ed's grandfather, Guy Golterman, produced grand opera and classical performances at the Coliseum, The Muny, and Kiel Opera House and Convention Hall. Golterman also inaugurated Cleveland Stadium with a grand opera in 1931. July Fourth, 1998, Ed wrote an impassioned defense of Kiel Opera House and sent it to the Urban Land Institute in Washington D.C. A ULI panel would soon come to St. Louis to *advise* on *what to do* with the Opera House. (Apparently re-opening the great theater to help bring back a downtown seemed too simple).

Kiel Opera House was *going down* to protect the Fox Theater on Grand Avenue and Kiel Center from what they feared as night time competition. Serving narrow *self-interests* hampers downtown revitalization. Citizens of the region, taxpayers and visitors deserve a better St. Louis, a better downtown. That means Kiel Opera House.

A newspaper columnist wrote of Ed: *He has been calling on the wrong people for two years*. Yes, and they are *all* the wrong people. Ed Golterman believed nothing written, said, or promised about Kiel Opera House. That has given him an edge on the battlefield. As Ed learned about Kiel Opera House *studies in the spring of 1998*, it became clear her enemies were *about to finish her off*. He said: No, and went to battle. Ten years later he is still fighting.

CHAPTER ONE

JUST ENOUGH HISTORY

Kiel Opera House in downtown St. Louis is closed. It houses one of the top five large natural theater/concert halls in the U.S. A deep and wide stage, rising orchestra pit, *close-in* balcony, and good acoustics make it very special. Kiel Opera House offers 70+ tracks for curtains, drops and flats, and perfect sight lines. And, it is *closed*.

Kiel also holds four smaller theater/auditoriums, a four-level foyer, grand staircase, 40,000 square feet of exposition space, and a massive special events and food and beverage area. It is in a downtown that has difficulty drawing *critical mass*.

1934, Gatti-Casazza, General Director of the Metropolitan Opera: *Kiel Opera House—with stage so magnificent no theater in the world surpasses it.* A functioning theater with *big* show capability was closed for renovation in 1991. It would reopen in 1994 or 1995 along with the new hockey arena for the St. Louis Blues.

Would any city in the country waste such a resource? One.

It remained closed into the new millennium to *protect* a large theater on Grand Avenue from *competition* and to keep Kiel Center *safe* from *competing* events at night. It remains closed because Civic Progress *decreed* it would remain closed. It remained closed through 2007. Owners of the hockey team who control the Opera House have lost money every year on the back end. They could make money on the front end.

In 1998, Civic Progress/Kiel Partners and collaborators launched *studies* aimed at gutting the Theater. The pretence was to turn Kiel into a museum or museums. A great deal of public and private money was *assigned* to this nefarious business. Did Chicago turn its Opera House into a museum when it needed upgrading? Did San Francisco *mothball* or destroy its quake-damaged Opera House? Did Detroit destroy an old downtown movie house and turn it into a museum or condos? Did Cleveland *gut* the theaters in Playhouse Square, or level them for parking?

In St. Louis a world-class civic performance, events, and cultural center remains *closed* when it should be contributing to downtown revitalization. Forget the word Opera. It's about jobs, revenue, income, and tourism. Attacks on Kiel Opera House may be or may not be unprecedented. But, the Kiel deal(s) have easily evolved into the City's dirtiest.

The Ambassador Theater was destroyed in 1995. The Arena would go in 1999. In this ten-years, chronicle, Kiel Opera House became more than a preservation *issue*. In 1998, *the powerful* put it back *in play* to finish it off. Others put it *in play* to save and re-open it. Both sides were very, very serious.

Bookend End 2007

Since the turn of the millennium, distrust greets nearly all *downtown* revitalization plans. Projects announced after elaborate studies are met with resistance, particularly when they call for heavy public support. Downtown Now's bid for State help to support infrastructure was *rejected* by the Legislature. Some Downtown promoters have fled; several to Portland. A tourism director went back to Indianapolis.

The *vultures* circle and craft new attacks on a helpless prey. The *museum* plots of the late 1990s became a 2003 plot to gut the theater and turn it into a school for performing arts. That plan came out of Grand Avenue. In 2005 an owner of the Fox weaseled his way into Don Breckenridge's plan to reopen Kiel and it never got off the ground.

Ownership of the Blues and control of the Opera House went from Civic Progress/Kiel Partners to Clark Enterprises, to Bill and Nancy Laurie, to Dave Checketts and Sports Capital Partners-World Wide. In January 2007, The Business Journal described Checkett's plans to reopen the Opera House. Mayor Slay had *no comment*. Development Director Barb Geisman had *no comment*. The Mayor's Chief of Staff Jeff Rainford had *no comment*. They have had no comment for 12 months.

The City has aggressively promoted a new ballpark, and Ballpark Village, a new casino, a Bottle District, more *dead* art on The Gateway Mall east of Tucker (12th Street) and John Danforth's plan to take some of the Arch grounds for development.

Kiel Opera House is still closed.

CHAPTER TWO

THE LEASE FROM HELL

1990 began the last decade of the millennium. St. Louisans are told the Arena on Oakland Avenue was inadequate and the Blues would move into a new civic center downtown. This would boost the economy and the culture of the core city. The plan was *sold* to those who had to *buy* it. Some believed. Some didn't. Kiel Center Development Corp. was formed. Its officers and attorneys began *shaping* the deal with the City. A two-year process was rushed to *train wreck* finalization late in 1992. It was *speeded* through the Board of Aldermen to *take advantage* of attractive bond rates. Some aldermen had not read the legislation.

The 10,000-seat Auditorium would be *demolished* and replaced with a 19,000-seat arena. The Opera House, with its 3,400 seat main theater, four smaller theater/auditoriums, and exposition hall would be renovated and re-opened. The combination would be operated as a civic entertainment, cultural, and sports center.

The new Kiel Center and restoring the Opera House would be funded *privately* by Civic Progress companies. Cost for the new Kiel Center was put at about $137 million. the City would spend about $37 million for demolition and infrastructure.

Master Lease (draft six) signed November 30, 1992

Larry Bushong, Director of The Land Clearance for Redevelopment Authority, signed for the City. H. Edwin Trusheim, President of Kiel Center Redevelopment Corp., signed for The Partners. Trusheim was CEO of General American Life and a member of Civic Progress. Also signing was

Secretary, Alfred H. Kerth III, a vice president of Fleishman Hillard Public Relations firm. F-H is Civic Progress primary PR firm.

Bryan Cave negotiated the lease on behalf of Kiel Partners. Chairman Walter Metcalfe, Jr. led their team. Metcalfe was a founder of Grand Center-midtown real estate and entertainment district. Bryan Cave is Grand Centers' law firm, and Civic Progress' law firm.

What the Lease Said, What the Lease Did

The lease called for *major replacement* of Kiel Auditorium. It called for destruction of the Convention Hall and parking garage, leaving the City without an indoor-events venue in the 10,000-seat range. (St. Charles would build and open a venue this size in 1998.) The lease called for *restoring* Kiel Opera House. *Restoring* meant tax breaks. Demolition of the Auditorium and building Kiel Center would cause *damage* to the Opera House, slicing off about 60 dressing rooms on the southwest corner and built walls dividing the two sides. Damage can be repaired. Walls can come down.

Kiel Center would encroach on the Opera House, taking space on several levels. It has used a 40,000 square foot exposition hall for storage and equipment supporting its operation. Limited repairs to the Opera House, referred to in the lease, *played out* to about *$2.5* million in damage repair and removal of asbestos.

The lease called for a new parking garage. Design and location of the parking garage is to serve only Kiel Center.

Truck Ramp/Load-In Tunnel

The new truck ramp and load-in tunnel on the west side of Kiel Center did *not* extend into or below the Opera House. The Opera House was deprived of load-in and sealed off from Kiel Center by bricks and mortar. St. Louisans were still being assured the Opera House would re-open.

Killed The Arena (no-compete)

The lease mandated The Arena on Oakland Avenue be prohibited from staging *for-admission* events. (The Arena was imploded February 27, 1999).

Tax Breaks Given for Civic Center, Civic Purpose and Use

Funding for the Kiel Center project included tax exempt bonds, preferred rates, and other considerations based on *historic* restoration and creation of a *civic center*. Nothing was restored, and there is nothing civic about Kiel Center. Lease Article 5.01 stipulated the City *has no approval rights regarding design or alterations.*

The City spent more than $15 million on site preparation, about $37 million overall. It receives revenue from the parking garage. On lease page 24 article 2.07, *insurance* was to be provided to take care of damage. However, there were no clauses in the lease to prevent damage to the Opera House nor to insure against damage to the Opera House. Civic Progress took *free reign* to do whatever they wanted. No one would stop them.

Certificate of Completion

In 1995, the City relieved Kiel Partners of financial obligation to restore the Opera House based on their spending $2.5 million on *repairs*. Bushong again *signed off* the fate *of* Kiel Opera House to sports franchise owners. Were there signs early on? Did anybody look at the signs and warn the people?

Bookend End 2007

This was a dishonorable business in 1991. It is a dishonorable business today. The Arena is gone. Kiel Convention Hall is gone. Kiel Opera House has been closed for 17 years: lost jobs, wages, benefits, gross and tax revenue, and waste of a major tourism draw.

Kiel Partners announced losses of $25 million during the first five years. Civic Progress companies bailed them out each year. They point to their great *civic* gesture in building Kiel Center and keeping the Blues in St. Louis. Bryan Cave's Walter Metcalfe warned the City *not to press the Opera House issue,* and expressed anger and indignation when reminded of their commitment: *We never promised.*

The Players

Trusheim retired from General American Life. He is a board member of the St. Louis Symphony and helps the Symphony raise money. Al Kerth's *roles* in attacks on the Opera House will be covered in several chapters. Bushong joined Husch and Eppenberger. Maureen McAvey took over as head of the St. Louis Development Corporation. She stayed three years and was succeeded by a retired Army engineer, then another.

The Old Post Office was designated downtown's historic restoration project via massive public subsidies. (It doesn't *threaten* the Fox Theater or Kiel Center). Bryan Cave continues to protect Grand Center, keeping Kiel Opera House out of downtown revitalization plans. The law firm's chairman, Don Lentz, is Chairman of Grand Center. Walter Metcalfe was one of Grand Center's first chairmen.

In October 1999, Bill and Nancy Laurie *bailed out* Kiel Partners. Nancy is daughter of Wal-Mart's Bud Walton. They bought the Blues and took control of Kiel Center and the Opera House. They showed no interest in re-opening the front part of the building. 'The House that Hull Built' (hockey star Brett Hull) has operated the last ten seasons without the Golden Brett who led Dallas to three Stanley Cup finals. The Blues can't get past the first round of the playoffs. Their operations lose *big* money. In 2000, Laurie sold the name *Kiel* and did not share proceeds with the City.

Savvis Center, formerly Kiel Center, never was a civic center. Mayors and administrations change—Schoemehl to Bosley to Harmon to Slay—but major decisions are not made at City Hall, including decisions on where St. Louis will present music, arts, and culture. While other downtowns are alive with new or restored and re-opened theaters, St. Louis wastes the best. Savvis Center seats 4,000 for concerts.

Kiel Opera House should have reopened before the turn of the millennium or certainly before 2004, the two-hundredth birthday of the City and one-hundredth anniversary of the World's Fair. *Post-Dispatch* managing editor Arnie Robbins told the author *we will report on the Opera House when something is done with it. That's too late, Arnie.* The Lauries *unloaded* the Blues in 2005 to Dave Checketts and Sports Capital Partners. 2006 and 2007 have come and gone. Savvis Center is now Scottrade Center.

Kiel Opera House is still closed.

CHAPTER THREE

OUTSIDE CONSULTANTS

St. Louisans should meet consultants at the airport and help them right
back on the plane

Author, KMOX Morning Meeting, Summit Restaurant, Spring, 1998.

Counter-culture spending

1 996–1999 more than $10 million was spent on studies designed in
whole or in part to destroy Kiel Opera House—its capacity to do large-
scale productions. That money went to consultants, urban planners,
architects, and other suppliers. Additional costs were incurred as City officials and employees of various bureaus and departments spent countless
hours on these initiatives.

Civic Progress, Kiel Partners/Clark Enterprises, Danforth Foundation,
and Union Station Partners kicked in a lot of money. If the money spent
on getting rid of Kiel Opera House had been spent to re-open it, it would
be open.

In St. Louis, studies are seldom probed or challenged *in advance*.
Afterward, reports and recommendations are often blasted as biased, sub-
jective, and wasteful. Use of consultants allows officials to delay action or
to shift *blame* to someone else. At least four City administrations have made
liberal use of *feasibility studies*.

Who benefits from studies?

- *City agencies* – staff and management thrive on the study-planning *process*. Studies are their *wellsprings*, their sustenance.

- *Architects and engineers* – are paid to conceptualize, to *render options and possibilities*.

- *Attorneys* – draft/review documents for hefty fees.

- *Economists* – do assessments of impacts for fees.

- *Advertising and public relations firms* – communicate studies and findings for fees.

- The *media* like studies. Reporters attend report meetings, do quick interviews, grab cups of coffee, and then are on to the next stories. Those who drink deepest from study *troughs* are consultants.

While St. Louis studies, other cities *do*: Cleveland renovated and opened its fourth theater downtown, restored a fifth, and re-opened a beautifully restored symphony hall.

Detroit turned an old downtown theater into the stunning Detroit Opera House. Pittsburgh opened two smaller theaters downtown, to partner with three large theaters. Chicago opens Shakespeare Theater at Navy Pier, re-opened the restored Goodwin, and operates more than a dozen theaters and concert halls downtown. Madison, Wisconsin built a $300 million downtown performing arts center, and added another theater.

Denver opened its performing arts center downtown. From ticket sales alone in 2001, DPAC delivered $2.2 million in tax revenue. The New Jersey Performing Arts Center sparked downtown Newark revitalization. Nashville operates a downtown performing arts center (three theaters and museum) and cross-promotes with other Nashville attractions. Seattle opened Benaroya Hall downtown in 1998, and is upgrading its Opera House. Benaroya Hall is home for six performing companies.

Outside consultants are brought to St. Louis to add *legitimacy* and *prestige*. They are a waste of time and money, and divert responsibility away from those who are responsible. They are brought to do dishonorable business. And this Kiel business is dishonorable business.

Bookend End 2007

In good and bad times, people travel. Theater, musical theater, and concert travelers spend more than a day and night in an area that offers *choices*. Cities that offer major live arts downtown generate business and revenue, year-round. St. Louis has destroyed or closed all but one of its downtown theaters. It modified The American so it cannot present *book* shows. The Fox *comes at* Kiel Opera House time after time with gut-it-for-re-use plans. Architects take dirty money *designing re-use*. They know there is no re-use plan. After commandeering a lot of private and public money to finish off Kiel and not succeeding, John Danforth is now seeking money to take over and commercialize some of the Arch grounds.

Kiel Opera House is still closed.

Chapter Four

The Urban Land Institute Study

March–July, 1998 Consultant fees: $75,000–$100,000

Plus Staff and Administrative Costs

City Employees, St. Louis Development Corporation

And ULI Task Force

February 1998 Comptroller Darlene Green announced formation of a task force to determine what do with Kiel Opera House. Green formed the 41-member ULI Task Force to develop background and provide *guidance* for a team of *experts* from the Urban Land Institute. *Post-Dispatch* articles alerted the author that the task force was heavily weighted against the Opera House.

More than half represented Kiel Partners/Civic Progress, Grand Center, the Fox, their attorneys, public relations firms, and financial institutions. More than 65% were *opposed* by words, actions, or lack of action to re-opening Kiel Opera House. Several members openly opposed its reopening for years. If all *other* task force member were *for* re-opening, it would still be a stacked deck. This was not a group to undertake an *objective study*. Kiel Opera House—closed and damaged—is surrounded by *wolves*.

- *Mark Sauer*—Chairman—President of The St. Louis Blues and Kiel Center. Kiel Partners refused to restore and reopen Kiel, and wants no *competition* in area, especially at night.

- *Co-Chair Maureen McAvey*, President, St. Louis Development Corp. Maureen had a fairly short stay in St. Louis. She had a business *history* with one or more of the ULI study panel (and perhaps a business *future*).

- Comptroller *Darlene Green*, protégé of former Mayor Freeman Bosley under whose administration the Convention Hall was destroyed, Opera House—closed and damaged. She holds the keys to the dormant Kiel Opera House, but Sauer controls it.

- *Steve Engelhardt*, Comptroller's Office, representing Green on the Task Force, working with task force members and with SLDC in preparing the *briefing* document.

- *Ann Ruwitch*, President of Grand Center. Most *rumors* about the condition of the Opera House originate at midtown: back stage is gone; bad acoustics will kill the Fox.

- *David Fay*, President of Fox Associates. David has been Grand Center's point man aimed at destroying Kiel for a decade.

- *Mike McMillan*, Alderman of the ward containing Grand Center and the Fox. He protects the interests of his constituents. However, his spot on this task force is a clear conflict of interest.

- *Attorney Steve Cousins*, Armstrong Teasdale. Board of Trustees of St. Louis Symphony at Grand Center, and Opera Theater in Webster Groves.

- *Rev. Lawrence Biondi*, SJ., President of St. Louis University on Grand Avenue.

- *Kathleen Brady*, St. Louis University on Grand Avenue.

- *Traci Johnson*, Mercantile Bank. Mercantile is a member of Kiel Partners-Civic Progress and a prime lender for Grand Center entities.

- *Richard Fleming*, President, Regional Commerce and Growth Association. *Dick* came from Denver where Denver Center for Performing Arts was the primary catalyst for downtown revitalization.

- *Mark Bernstein*, Repertory Theater of Webster Groves. The Rep co-produces shows with the Fox.

- *Joanne LaSala*, President, St. Louis 2004. Her boss, John Danforth, does not want *anything to compete* with Grand Center. Joanne was formerly with Fleishman-Hillard. She represents Danforth. Danforth represents Grand Avenue.

- *Al Kerth III Fleishman-Hillard*, spokesperson for Civic Progress, Kiel Center during development. Kerth signed the 1992 lease that destroyed Kiel Auditorium, damaged the Opera House and eliminated the Arena on *no-compete* clauses. He was quoted in 1994 in promising the Kiel Opera House *would be done first class.*

- *Bob Bedell*, President of the St. Louis Convention and Visitors Commission. SLCVC is charged with bringing tourists and conventions to St. Louis. Downtown theater and cultural tourism helps revitalize downtowns.

- *Valerie Patton*, NationsBank. Civic Progress (Has become Bank of America.)

- *Wil Gregory*, Downtown Partnership. Partnership is committed to protecting Grand Center and the Fox.

- *Dan Krasnoff*, St. Louis Development Corporation. He drafted the ULI panel *briefing* document that will instruct consultants to find *any other use but music* for the Opera House. The document will understate market population.

- *Steve Miller*, Union Station Partners. Union Station would be the primary benefactor of a re-opened Kiel Opera House.

- *Ron Himes*, Black Rep. The Black Repertory Theater is in Grand Center.

- *Dr. Robert Archibald*, The History Museum in Forest Park. In the midst of a major fund raising effort and expansion. Protecting his endowments *turf*?

- *Jill McGuire*, Regional Arts Commission. This agency is in Grand Center. Jill's vision for arts and entertainment in St. Louis is broader than Grand Center.

- *Wayman Smith*, Anheuser-Busch. A-B is a member of Kiel Partners/Clark Enterprises/Civic Progress.

- *Steve Schankman*, Contemporary Productions. Owns Riverport Amphitheater in Earth City. Steve offered to buy Opera House in the early '90s. *Excellent theater/concert hall.*

- *Norman Seay*, UMSL. University of Missouri-St. Louis. UMSL is building its own performing arts center. Chancellor Touhill is ex-officio, Civic Progress.

- *Chester Hines*, Mayor's Office. the City is periodically warned not to pursue action against Civic Progress to re-open the Opera House.

- *Jonathan Kleinbard*, Missouri Botanical Gardens. In the Shaw neighborhood. What is he doing on a task force deciding the future of a major downtown performing arts center?

- Fourth Ward Alderwoman *Marit Clark*. Downtown St. Louis needs *energized* redevelopment.

- *Keith Alper*, Creative Producers Group: Past President of The Advertising Club of Greater St. Louis. Keith operates a multi-media business and marketing firm.

- Other members of the Task Force: Joy Burns, YWCA; Carolyn Seward, Better Family Life; Dr. Glen Holt, St. Louis Public Library; Yvonne Days, Ida Woolfork and Bob Nordman, St. Louis Public Schools; Paul Weiss, Hot Locust Cantina; Dean Weese, Washington University; Carolyn Toft, Landmarks Association; Dr. Donald Suggs, St. Louis American; Tom Gray, Velvet Lounge.

Only two performing groups were represented: The Repertory Theater of Webster Groves and The Black Rep in Grand Center. No dance companies, orchestras, festivals, or events planners were on the Task Force. There was no one from The Alliance of Mid-Sized Theaters, in need of performing space. Also missing is Charles MacKay, Opera Theater. Charles could have talked about the 30% increase in grand opera attendance during the 1990s and reminded St. Louis Kiel Opera House is a superb theater.

The Municipal Theater in Forest Park is not represented. The Muny should be helping its downtown *cousin,* with short winter seasons. Sally Bliss, Director of Dance St. Louis, was not included. Sally *would use the Opera House in a minute.* Large stage makes it ideal for dance. Sarah Bryan Miller, classical music critic of the *Post-Dispatch,* was not included. Sarah has lamented the loss of the large *natural sound* theaters.

Symphony Conductor Hans Vonk was not involved. Many Symphony members would like to perform again at Kiel, the Symphony's home for 32 years. There were no representatives from southern Illinois—cultural or business—who could talk about the *regional* value of Kiel. Tens of thousands of southern Illinois residents patronize sporting events in downtown St. Louis. Would not some come to Kiel? Six MetroLink lines from Illinois funnel into downtown and drop off across from Kiel Center.

There would be no voice to tell how other cities were using cultural and entertainment venues help revitalize downtowns. No one on the task force would suggest that a re-opened Opera House complex would be *good business,* that the cost of renovation could be offset by naming, sponsoring, licensing. Performing arts centers are *hot* naming and endowment draws. Former Kiel manager Bruce Sommer was not part of the task force. He literally screamed in the mid 1980s that it *just needed marketing.* Marketing Kiel ended in the 1980s as Mayor Vince Schoemehl promised the restorers of the Fox Theater they would never have to *worry* about Kiel.

No senior citizens or senior citizens groups were represented. Seniors are the fastest growing population segment. Senior citizens seek entertainment, and will travel for entertainment. Who was left *off* the task force is as revealing as who was included.

The Study Process

February–July, They held meetings to prepare a *briefing* document for the visiting ULI panel. The document would *pre-condition* the panel toward gutting the Opera House for *re-use.* The Comptroller began talking about preserving the architectural integrity of the building. She likely meant preserving only the exterior.

Task Force Meetings

Meetings were held in a *small* conference room in Kiel Center. They were *open* to the public, but poorly publicized. Weekday afternoons made it difficult. The time seemed also inconvenient for task force members, reflected in light turnout.

Krasnoff assembled The *briefing document.* When completed it was sent to the eight members of The ULI panel. It was never shared with the public.

Briefing Document Handcuffs Consultants

Kiel Opera House must not *cannibalize* any other theaters, meaning it must not *compete* with the Fox, or with a proposed theater at UMSL. When The Allen was restored and re-opened in Cleveland did it *cannibalize* the other three theaters in Playhouse Square? Kennedy Center is considering a fourth theater. Do the other three fear a fourth? Did Opryland fear it would be *cannibalized* by Tennessee Performing Arts Center?

The Ethics of Consulting

Would a team of doctors allow a patient to tell them how to diagnose and treat? Would an attorney allow a client to set parameters for case development? The Study sponsors told the ULI panel what to recommend and paid them to do so. Bryan Cave has an office in Washington D.C. not Far from the Urban Land Institute.

ULI Kiel Opera House ULI Panel

- *Charles Kendrick, Jr.*, Managing Director, Clarion Ventures, LLC, Boston. (Maureen McAvey came to St. Louis from Boston)

- *Robert Bailey*, AMS Planning and Research, Petaluma, CA. In June 1998, Bailey's firm completed a major preliminary study on the proposed performing arts center on The University of Missouri-St. Louis campus. *Conflict of Interest*

- *Dan Spikes*, VP–Restaurant Development, Black Entertainment TV. Washington, D.C.

- *Ranne Warner*, President Centros Properties USA, Inc. Boston.

- *Linda S. Congleton*, Linda S. Congleton and Associates, Irvine, CA.

- *Max Bond*, Davis Brody Bond, New York, NY.

- *James Porter.* Saltine and Porter Architects, Los Angeles, CA.

- *Anne Warhover*, Economic Development Services, Downtown Denver Partnership

ULI PANEL IN ST. LOUIS—JUNE 19-22, 1998

Panel members would meet with sponsors, tour the Opera House, interview *interested* parties, and deliver a report, all within three days.

Sunday, July 19. Panel members arrived, had dinner with sponsors of the study, city officials and other interested parties at the Fox Theater on Grand Avenue.

Monday, July 20. Panel toured Opera House and interviewed so-called area business, and arts leaders and a few citizens.

Interviews continued into Tuesday. Warhover interviewed the author. He walked her through a 32-page business plan that called for multi use, with costs shared by several responsible parties. He gave her several copies of the text as well as the plan on videotape for the convenience of the panel. He urged the panel to recommend restoration and re-opening of the Opera House for cultural and economic benefits. The Panel never acknowledged receipt of his plan.

The author hand-delivered copies to: the Mayor's Office, Comptroller Green, Aldermanic President Slay, City Treasurer Williams, RCGA, Danforth Foundation, St. Louis Business Journal, Post-Dispatch, Downtown Now, and Kiel Partners. He sent a copy to developer Don Breckenridge, a pretty innovative St. Louisan.

Wednesday, July 21. The panel reported to the sponsors, then to the public at an open meeting in the Kennedy Conference Room, City Hall. About 75 were on hand: Task force members, City officials, consultants, the public and the media. Charlie Kendrick explained the agenda. He brought members of the panel up to present segments of the report. They were *mechanical*, as if their report had been set in slow drying concrete. How do you energize dishonorable work?

A very costly study and a three-day show culminated with the panel recommending *gutting* Kiel Opera House and turning it into a museum, and to move fairly quickly.

Panel Findings/Recommendations (condensed)

1. Overwhelming obstacle to re-opening is the *slow* growth of the market. No. That's an overwhelming reason *to* re-open it, to help *grow* the market. Other cities *grow* downtowns by providing choices

in entertainment and cultural. St. Louis wants to revive its down-town. Few cities have a downtown resource like Kiel Opera House.

2. City population is falling, can't support another large theater.
    City population is not the true market. Regional population is up
    slightly, now about 2.6 million. Residents on both sides of the river
    attend sporting events downtown. St. Louis is at the east/west
    and north/south major travel routes. Downtown does not offer
    one functioning major indoor theater for year 'round operation. A
    Metro station is a block away. Four thousand more hotel rooms are
    being planned for downtown St. Louis.

3. Turn it into a Smithsonian satellite or Blues/Jazz museum. No.
    Museums burden taxpayers. They are mostly day-trip attractions.
    Downtown St. Louis needs attractions that draw people at night,
    and for overnight stays.

4. Establish a $25 million trust fund to do the *dirty work*. the City,
    Kiel Partners, St. Louis 2004, RCGA, and NationsBank would pay
    for gutting the theater for *re-use and redevelopment*. No. Trust fund
    should fund its preparation for re-opening.

5. There should be separate ownership from Kiel Center/Kiel
    Partners. Yes. The sports-owners showed no interest, denied
    responsibility. Operations should be separate. New owner/operator
    for Opera House is essential.

Bailey (the double-dipper) said there was no leadership to re-open the Opera House. (Bailey's firm in Irvine is cashing checks from UMSL). Kendrick thanked the panel and told the public to keep comments short—*no speeches.* He came here to tell us to destroy one of the world's finest theaters and is telling us how to react? Asshole. Spikes told us to *control our emotions.* He comes from D.C. to tell us to destroy a theater superior to any theater in D.C.? Asshole. Fifteen citizens took turns at the microphone. They quietly and intelligently *dismantled* the panel's assessment and recommendations.

Citizens blasted the panel for not understating the market and market potential. The Arts and Education Council, Pat Rich, said their figures were wrong. Historian H. Russell Carter communicated how Seattle, Denver, and Cleveland provide more theater choices, and draw more people. Pastor Mike Tooley, Centenary United Methodist Church, said downtown is dead at night. And a re-opened Opera House will bring life and energy. Jeff Stewart,

Windsor Theater Group, said Grand Center doesn't seem to care about small theater companies who need performing space. The author: Museums-on-every-corner will not generate the energy or excitement Downtown needs.

This slam-dunk was blocked.

Panel members scowled. Sauer. Green, Krasnoff, Englehardt squirmed. Ruwitch left early. Turning a great theater into a museum, using one cultural entity to destroy another, is dishonorable business. Paying consultants to do dishonorable business is dishonorable business. The panel listened for 30 minutes. Comptroller Green thanked them. Charlie and his crew gave a few interviews, closed their brief cases, picked up their checks, and headed for the airport. *Thanks, Charlie, don't come back.*

Leaders in other cities help arts beget arts: the Benaroyas in Seattle; the Junior League and Cleveland Foundation in Cleveland; dynamic mayors in Detroit, Nashville and Memphis. Fair competition keeps prices reasonable, quality up, and gives people more reasons to come to a city and to its downtown.

In St. Louis Arts *kill* Arts. Cultural, business and civic *non-leaders* sacrifice Kiel Opera House to protect Grand Center. They do not have the courage to do it directly. The announced $75,000–$100,000 consultant's fee was paid primarily by Kiel Partners/Clark Enterprises. Robert Bailey's participation was a clear conflict of interest. The whole ULI exercise was laced with conflicts of interest.

Friday, July 24, The *Post-Dispatch* blistered ULI panel recommendations, describing the study as *flawed* and *self-serving.* It urged the Task Force to table recommendations until they have better facts, figures and answers from Clark Enterprises. The Post called on Kiel Partners to meet their obligation to restore and re-open Kiel Opera House. *Riverfront Times* Publisher Ray Hartmann described Civic Progress/Kiel Partners' promise to reopen the Opera House as *Unqualified.* Letters to editors expressed outrage with the findings of the *outside* consultants, and the continued waste of Kiel.

Mark Sauer stuck to the Kiel Partners' script: *We never promised to re-open it, was a public relations misunderstanding.* We have the Fox and will have the theater on the campus of UMSL. Who is *we,* Sauer? You speak only for you bosses.

JULY 29. FINAL TASK FORCE MEETING

The *wolves* circle once more. But, they are also encircled. Task force members filled into the small conference room in Kiel Center. They took their seats around the conference table, and were surrounded by 30 St. Louisans. It was the largest turnout of task force members and of the public. There was little discussion of the Report. It had been sliced and diced by the public and the media. No panel member suggested adopting the recommendations.

Jill McGuire called the Study absolutely incomplete and the consultants' presentation *a little arrogant*. She disputed the conclusion that St. Louis could not support multiple venues. Mark Sauer talked about costs of repairs, maintenance and inspections. He did not refer to the consultants' recommendations. David Fay admitted that everyone knew his position—*Opera House should go away*. Sauer opened it up for public comments.

Jennifer Grotpeter, granddaughter of a Kiel architect, said she would much prefer enjoying music in the Opera House than at the Fox. She looked at Sauer then at Fay. Others commented that Kiel would provide performance space, and space for artists to display their works. *Look at what other cities are doing. It won't hurt Grand Avenue. Fits perfectly with downtown revitalization. Choices grow great cities.* Stop wasting this resource. If you want people downtown offer more attractions.

Darlene Green ended the meeting: *It looks like there is still hope for the Opera House*. She seemed relieved The ULI experience was over. The task force adjourned and dissolved *without* adopting the panel recommendations. The people had actually won. However, Mark Schlinkmann's P-D article did not mention the public comments. He quoted only task force members. The *war correspondent* did not report the *victory*.

The ULI matter was dishonorable business. The wolves circled again, spent a lot of money, and brought in consultants for the *song and dance*. The people said: *get the hook*. Minimum cost—$100,000 to $500,000. But, what is the price for destroying credibility?

Saturday August 8th *St. Louis Post-Dispatch:*

"I see no competition between UMSL performing arts center and facilities in city of St. Louis. Issue is: will a fully functional Kiel Opera House undermine the city's investment in Grand Center."

Lowell Girardier, Florissant.

"I got the distinct impression everyone there (the final task force meeting) favored moving forward, now."

Jeff Stewart, Windsor Theater Group.

"The City met its deal. Kiel Partners needs to meet theirs."

Jay Rosloff.

"Why is it St. Louis forces always hire idiots to tell us how to think."

Joseph O. Fisher, Richmond Heights.

"ULI Panel recommended a death squad for the Opera House—2004, the RCGA, Kiel Partners and NationsBank."

The Author.

August 14, 1998 *Post-Dispatch* editorial—*A Promise is a Promise*

Nothing has altered Kiel Partners' obligation to refurbish Kiel. The people of St. Louis should not have to lose a beloved venue simply because other theaters worry that they might lose business. The Post is on it now: editorials, articles, commentaries, letters. Columnist Greg Freeman writes about the multiple uses of the Opera House. Sports writer Bernie Miklasz wrote simply: *Free the Opera House.*

Where are the investigative reporters: Challenging the *stacked deck, nailing* sponsors for their self-interests, taking apart the biased briefing document, pointing out Bailey's conflict-of-interest, and uncovering others? If it smelled bad at the end, perhaps it smelled bad at the beginning. Citizens should *not* have to do investigative reporting. This is the responsibility of the media and of law enforcement agencies.

The Riverfront Times said The ULI study skirted the fundamental issue of The Kiel Center owner's pledge to renovate and reopen the Kiel Opera House. D. J. Wilson writes: *a little public outcry* might help. The RFT began a series of in-depth articles on the state of downtown plans, the studies, the delays and the power of Civic Progress. And they are printing more letters from the people on the Opera House situation.

The *Suburban Journals* increase coverage. St. Louis Core and Intermission are covering the Opera House matter. *The Jewish Light, Il Pensiero, St. Louis Times* write of the value of Kiel. The *St. Louis Journalism Review* frequently exposes the power and control of Civic Progress. The *Webster-Kirkwood Times* did a feature on a Kirkwood resident and his *mission.* Reporters were picking up on some kind of momentum. There were more and more reports on the Opera House on talk shows and in newscasts.

Channel 30's Don Marsh did a *meaty* expose in late 1998. KMOX, KTRS and WIL liberally covered efforts of those advocating re-opening Kiel.

Mayor Harmon tried to see if the City could take legal action to force Kiel Partners to re-open Kiel. City Counselor Eric Banks, amid differences of opinion in his department, recommended against suing. Banks cited the 1994 *certificate of completion*. The Mayor said the City basically *signed away* its rights. How can City officials sign away rights to a building owned by the people? How can they let the Opera House die to ease the anxiety of the owners of the Fox Theater. Protect and use your assets.

St. Louis studies are predictable and vulnerable to attack. Those who *pay* for the studies *dictate* the results. The ULI consultants were not credible. Citizen input is *illusionary*. All decisions are made behind closed doors. Public meetings give citizens the illusion that they participate. Officials hide behind studies to delay action, take the wrong action, and blame the consultants if their course of action fails. Study sponsors are confident that no one will be interested enough to look closely. They were wrong.

Re-Use, Architectural Integrity–Red Flags

At least one reporter might have picked up on re-use vs. re-opening. Had Darlene Green been persuaded the Opera House should not reopen as a theater? Did the comptroller view the architectural integrity of the building as the exterior only?

> June 7, 1998
> Mark Sauer and Maureen McAvey—Co-Chairs
> Task Force Members
> And ULI Panel
>
> Architectural Integrity
>
> I believe the latest Kiel Opera House committee is charged with finding ways to preserve the *Architectural Integrity* of the Kiel Opera House or building. If this is fairly close, then we all need to understand that it is impossible to *separate* the architectural integrity of Kiel Opera House from *music*. In 1928–29, Guy Golterman traveled to Europe, visited and studied nearly 30 grand opera houses in France,

Germany, Italy and Australia and contracted European opera stars, all in preparation for Kiel Opera House.

(The dream of a great indoor opera house dated back to the opening of The Municipal Theater in Forest Park in 1917—a dream kept alive through world war and recessions by Henry Kiel, Nelson Cunliff, Golterman, and all lovers of good music in St. Louis).

Golterman's research in Europe combined with the architect's renderings (I don't know who the architect was) and the unparalleled construction (perhaps by Henry Kiel's construction company and others) gave St. Louis the finest Opera House in the Country, for all types of musical presentations.

We can't separate the architectural integrity or any other integrity connected with Kiel Opera House from the theater/concert hall, from the music. It is not a museum. It is not a school. That would be like trying to preserve the architectural integrity of Busch Stadium, but no baseball. Or, the architectural integrity of Carnegie Hall or the Metropolitan Opera House, but turning them into museums, offices, shops or parking garages.

The Author
cc: Mayor Harmon, John Hoal, Gene Mackey, Steve Schankman.

Dishonorable work is allowed to run its course and is then *fed* to the people as valid, objective and legitimate. Action is planned and taken to quickly move toward the *objectives* of the study. Gutting the Opera House could have begun quickly on the *promise* of something that may or may not ever happen. With little protection from City officials, the media, or law enforcement agencies, the people must get in the game a little *earlier*.

Parallel Universe—Same time frame as ULI study. February–July, 1998

The author was invited to take part in a program on KMOX radio, hosted by Charlie Brennan, originating from The Summit Restaurant downtown, and included Ray Hartmann, then publisher of *The Riverfront Times*. I stated that

Kiel Opera House was being kept closed to *protect* the Fox and Kiel Center's monopolies and that all outside consultants should be stopped at the airport.

Ray said it was Kiel Partner's responsibility to renovate and reopen Kiel Opera House as promised. I said the City should take it away from Kiel Partners and have another group restore and reopen it. Kiel Partners would still have to put some money on the table. The audience at the Summit was supportive, from a nostalgic standpoint.

At the Summit, I connected with Russ Carter, a theater expert, historian and advocate for re-opening Kiel. Russell, Jeff and Elle Stewart and I formed the nucleus of the support group but were quickly joined by others. (Kiel For Performing Arts would be incorporated in September 1998). St. Louis Core, a downtown area *upbeat* newspaper and Intermission covered our efforts. Action begat coverage begat interest begat action. We gave talks, anywhere and to anyone. People began to read and listen.

Bookend End 2007

McAvey resigned before the end of the ULI fiasco. In 2000, David Fay left the Fox in a contract dispute. Then... in February, Joanne LaSala resigned as President of St. Louis 2004 and Ann Ruwitch resigned as President of Grand Center in March. Al Kerth would engage in more attempts to dispose of Kiel. Steve Engelhardt pushed the museums idea until he resigned in May. Krasnoff quit SLDC in June, taking a job with St. Louis County. Steve Schankman said he had been approached to help turn Kiel into a Blues/Jazz museum but declined. ULI Panel briefing document is still on file at SLDC

Dick Fleming, RCGA, *hawked* a new ballpark for the Cardinals and now-ballpark village. He *sells* whatever Civic Progress and John Danforth tell him to *sell*.

Alderwoman Clark left the Board and is practicing law in Clayton. Norman Seay retired from UMSL. Comptroller Green blocks all attempts to re-open Kiel. She quickly authorized $250 million in bonds for a replacement ballpark for the Cardinals.

Bob Bedell left the Convention and Visitors Commission and went back to Indianapolis. Steve Miller, Union Station Partners, provided financial support for the Smithsonian satellite idea. Nineteenth Ward Alderman Mike McMillan is now License Collector.

Mark Sauer stonewalled all attempts to reopen Kiel

Kiel Partners/Clark Enterprises sold the Blues to Bill and Nancy Laurie (Wal-Mart). They wasted the Opera House for five years then sold the Blues to Dave Checketts and his investors.

Kiel Opera House is still closed.

CHAPTER FIVE

ST. LOUIS 2004 CULTURAL ASSESSMENTS STUDY

46-Member Task Force
Funding: St. Louis 2004 and Others
John Danforth: *We want nothing to compete with Grand Center*
JoAnne LaSala, President, St. Louis 2004
June 1997–December 1998 $100,000 to Consultant
Another $200,000 2004 salaries—Marvin Anderson and Shaughnessy
   Daniels,
2004 staff, city officials and employees (no estimate)
Consultant Victor Gotesman, Theater Projects Consultants. Ridgefield, Conn.
Gotesman also consulted on UMSL's theater project.

The 1904 World's Fair was a remarkable achievement but St. Louis is often accused of *hanging on to the past*. 2004 seems like a good *peg* on which to mount an effort to improve St. Louis. In 1996, John Danforth created St. Louis 2004 and seed funded it through his Foundation. The goal: major improvements in St. Louis by 2004. 2004 has an office in One Met Square. The staff: former staffers at Fleishman-Hillard public relations agency, city departments and some young *blood*. Big paychecks.

June, 1997–December 1998, St. Louis 2004 conducted its own cultural assessment study. Bob Archibald chaired the group which was weighted three to one museum and art interests over performing arts, and was Grand Center *dominated*.

Grand Center Representatives

Arts and Education Council–Pat Rich

Regional Arts Commission–Jill McGuire

St. Louis Symphony–Bruce Coppock and Jim Mann

St. Louis Black Rep–Ron Himes, Shay Wafer

Dance St. Louis–Sally Bliss, Annelise Mertz

Urban League-Vaughn Cultural–Cookie Jordon

KETC Channel 9–Ted Garcia

Arts Mgt. Instructor, St. Louis University–Joanne Kohn

TNT–Agnes Wilcox

Grand Center–President Ann Rewitch came in and out in participating

Museums/Silent Arts Institutions

Missouri Historical Society–Bob Archibald and Marsha Bray

Arts Academy of Bharata–Vipin B. Bhatt

Forum for Contemporary Art–Betsy Millard

Artmart–Keith Baizer

School of Art, Washington U.–Joe Deal, Dean and Pat Schucard, Professor.

Washington U. Art History and Archaeology–Chairman Mark Weil and Andrea Hawkins, Assistant Professor

Craft Alliance–Sharon McPherron, Executive Director

St. Peters Cultural Arts Center

Missouri African American Cultural Initiative

Midwest Museums Conference

Performing Companies/Theaters

The New Theater

St. Louis Symphony

Opera Theater–Charles McKay (looking at Grand Center)

Repertory Theater of Webster Groves–Steve Woolf and Mark Bernstein (ULI)

Gash-Voigt Dance Company

Black Repertory Theater

Metro Theater–Carol North

Dance St. Louis–Sally Bliss

The Uppity Theater Company–Joan Lipkin

Taproots School of the Arts–Melanie Daniels, Gretchen Beck

Metro Theater Co.–Joan Brichetti

Florissant Civic Center Theater–Gary Gaydos, Manager

Others

Monsanto Fund–Lynn Barth. *Don't waste your time applying for a grant—* May of 1998.

Peter Sargent, Dean, Webster University College of Fine Arts.

Lynda Milne, Mo. Citizens for the Arts; Michael Bouman, Missouri Humanities Council; Rich Walker Arts and Issues, SIU-E; Tulia Hamilton, St. Louis Community Foundation; Bill Finnie, Consultant; Nancy Margulies.

No one representing downtown revitalization interests or who could talk about the value of Kiel Opera House or how other cities are using new and renovated old theaters to help spark downtown rebirth. No one from the tourism industry.

ULI–2004 Studies–Similarities, *Perceived* Differences

Grand Center influenced the 2004 study even more heavily than the ULI study.

Several of the public meetings were held in Grand Center including the final meeting.

In the ULI study there was little citizen input. We just showed up. Louis 2004 study managers invited cultural leaders, board members, and citizens to meetings. The topics and the discussions were *highly controlled*.

The *illusion* was given that public input is desired and considered. If meeting facilitators are skilled, they *pull it off*. If not, they tip their hands and discredit their own efforts. I presented a multi-use business plan for the Opera House to a 2004 staffer. He said *people would not go back to the Opera House because of the hockey crowd*. I thanked him for his time and left. Joanne LaSala said the 2004 study would not involve Kiel Opera House, and referred me to Downtown Now. Not true. When the ULI study flopped, the fate of Kiel was quickly *handed off* to the 2004 committee and consultant.

What the 2004 Cultural Study ignored:

Downtown Now consultants address a dead area along Market Street between Union Station and Tucker Boulevard. It's dead because Kiel Opera House, on Market between 14th and 15th, is closed. The Post's Greg Freeman sees multiple civic and cultural uses for Kiel. *The building would bring much needed color to an otherwise dull area.* Aldermanic President Francis Slay said the Opera House is in our critical mass area and must be reopened. Consultant Victor Gotesman was not listening.

DECEMBER 22, 1998. PUBLIC MEETING, GRANDEL THEATER, REPORT ON 2004 CULTURAL ASSESSMENTS STUDY

Gotesman seemed *uninformed* about Kiel, the market, downtown, or anything beyond Grand Center. He would quickly dismiss the Opera House, move on to more important matters, collect his fees and leave town. He didn't bank on Russ Carter, Joe Dubuque or Peter Vaccaro. Gotesman was not prepared. They took him apart.

2004 Study findings and recommendations:

1. Build a 1200–1800 seat theater in Grand Center for Fox Associates.

2. Arts Community has no leadership. St. Louis needs an arts czar.

4. Kiel Opera House is not needed—would cost too much to re-open.

What was too much? He didn't know. All reasonable costs are in the $35 million to $45 million range. Chicago spent $100 million restoring The Lyric Opera House.

San Francisco raised $88 million to upgrade its quake-damaged Opera House. Benaroya Hall cost $121 million in Seattle. Philadelphia spent $247 million on a two-theater downtown performing arts center.

Fox Associates has promised to use the UMSL performing arts center 85 dates a year. Gotesman is consulting on that project. Kiel offers the 3,500 seat main theater and four smaller theater/auditoriums.

5. *St. Louis can't support more than one large theater.*

A region of 2.6 million, in mid America, trying to revitalize its core, on major east/west, north/south travel routes cannot support more than one large theater?

Another consultant tells St. Louis it is a small town. He used nearly the same words Bailey used in The ULI study. LaSala said they gave Gotesman *no marching orders* on the Opera House but her boss John Danforth says *nothing should compete with Grand Center.* Gotesman said the Opera House should *not* re-open.

Was Gotesman given the same briefing document as The ULI Panel? Was Grand Center to be the total focus. Participants from outside the city felt ignored.

"The disappointing aspects of this study are the absence of ideas for downtown and the discounting of Kiel as a viable performing arts venue. As we struggle to revitalize downtown—our region's center of gravity. *It is shortsighted to see a plan almost entirely focused on Grand Center.* St. Louis Post-Dispatch Editorial December 13, 1998.

In July, 2000 a member of the 2004 task force from St. Charles County shared:

"*I felt somehow the results were guided by someone other* than the presenters of the study group. (John Danforth?) *I remember saying to the committee that we were not asked to make a judgment on the Opera House. They just did it. Unless they were guided by someone else.*"

Bookend End 2007

The Players

Grand Center controlled the St. Louis 2004 study through John Danforth. Danforth confirmed in May 2000, *we don't want anything to compete with Grand Center.* Bryan Cave is his law firm. Bryan Cave's Chairman is Grand Center's Chairman. Tall Jack funds studies to get ride of Kiel to protect the Fox. This is not hard to figure out.

LaSala resigned from 2004, shortly after the study. Peter Sortino succeeded LaSala as President of 2004. Archibald went back to Forest Park and his museum. So much for performing arts helping revitalize downtown St. Louis. Through St. Louis 2004 and his Foundation, Danforth has spent more than a million dollars to dispose of a great theater.

Pat Rich left Arts and Education Council. Briccetti left Metro Theater. Sargent and Bernstein went back to Webster Groves. Wilcox closed TNT. Bernstein and Woolf of the Rep. continue to collaborate with the Fox and Grand Center. Mark Sauer says he accepts the findings of the study. Gotesman is consulting somewhere. Don't come back.

(In 1996, the Fox Theater and Fox Associates did their own study of what to do with Kiel Opera House. Their recommendation was to keep the exterior and turn the inside into parking.)

In 2001, Tom Turner resigned as President and CEO of Grand Center and *fled* to Portland, saying he had *no position* on Kiel Opera House. Former Mayor Vince Schoemehl replaced him. Those determined to get rid of the Opera House are still at it. Investigations would uncover agreements to kill the Opera House.

Kiel Opera House is still closed.

Chapter Six

Smithsonian Satellite Ploy

(What the people don't know won't hurt them, and might help us)

Let's Turn the Opera House Into A Museum

"No, we have an overabundance of museums and four on the drawing boards. Downtown needs the energy and dynamics of theater, especially at night."

St. Louis Museum Corporation, affiliated with the Smithsonian

Initial Study Cost $300,000 Funded by The Danforth Foundation,

Union Station Partners, and Kiel Partners

Real Estate Attorney Alan Bornstein, Sonnenschein Nath and Rosenthal

Developer *Richard Baron*

Mark Sauer, Clark Enterprises/Kiel Partners, ULI Co-Chair.

Steve Miller, Union Station Partners, ULI Task Force

Donna Laidlaw, Union Station Partners

Al Kerth III, ULI Task Force, PR Counsel to Civic Progress

Bruce Anderson, Danforth Foundation

For The Smithsonian:

Michael Carrigan, Director of Affiliations and Margaret Pulles, Affiliations Coordinator.

Museum Consultants: Lord Cultural Resources, Toronto, Canada.

Kiel Partners complain they lose money on Kiel Center and on the Blues, so they cannot re-open the Opera House. However, they can find $$$$$$ for studies to destroy it.

SMITHSONIAN STUDIES AND PLANS

Spring 1998–end October 1999, St. Louisans were told Kiel Opera House was being considered by the Smithsonian as a location for a satellite. Some were impressed that our downtown could have a Smithsonian branch. Others felt we had enough museums and needed more excitement downtown. Whatever the reaction in St. Louis nothing is as it seems. Smithsonian satellite idea for Kiel Opera House was the *carrot* extended to St. Louisans for their passive acceptance of the final destruction of the Opera House.

Dazzle 'em while you economically and culturally *rape* 'em, again. Give them a cultural *high* while you do a cultural *low*. As the story goes....

Alan Bornstein was bicycling downtown and passed Al Kerth, also on a bike, or, they were riding together. They chatted and imagined downtown a *bustling* place with lots of people and wondered what dramatic project might help make that happen.

Bornstein, as the story goes, learned The Smithsonian was talking with 17 cities about parceling out stored items. Kerth rode over to Kiel Center or perhaps to One Met Square with *another way to get rid of the Opera House.* The Danforth Foundation said *yes* and put $100,000 on the table. Union Station Partners put up $100,000 and Clark Enterprises/Kiel Partners $100,000 for another opportunity to *get rid* of Kiel.

Baron and Bornstein sent an architect into the Opera House to *render* its destruction. The Opera House as a possible Smithsonian Satellite remained before the people from early 1998 until late 1999. Whether or not The Smithsonian ever came to St. Louis the *gang* could use that prospect to kill Kiel Opera House. Bornstein, Baron, Danforth, Sauer, Miller, and Kerth would give Grand Avenue its great *trophy*. In the spring of 1998 The *Post-*

Dispatch reported The St. Louis Museum Corporation affiliated with the Smithsonian Institution was considering Downtown St. Louis and the Kiel Opera House as a possible location for a Smithsonian *presence* in St. Louis.

May 19, 1998

Mr. Alan Bornstein—Attorney at Law
(St. Louis Museum Corp.
1 Metropolitan. Square
St. Louis, MO. 63102)

Dear Alan,

We should all ride bicycles more. Our best ideas do not come in meetings, or through surveys. Congratulations on an innovative individual step to revive culture in downtown St. Louis. It is much needed.

As you look at the Opera House complex, look at the Exposition Hall, built for exhibits. With ground-level entrance, art lovers of all ages would have easy access to the Smithsonian-West. It is exhibit space. Upstairs, imagine The Metropolitan Opera of New York collaborating with us to operate the first and only Regional Metropolitan Opera Company in the Country.

The Smithson and The MET, in the same facility? No city would have this blockbuster. We would immediately leapfrog Chicago as the cultural center of the mid west (and we *owe* Chicago a few).

If you decide Cupples Station or another downtown space is more appropriate, St. Louis would still be the only city in the country with a MET/Smithsonian combination.

If I can assist your efforts with the SMITHSONIAN, how about helping me get our 'glorious music house reopened? There has never been such an exciting combination, anywhere.

The Author

Bornstein ducked all approaches to discuss cooperative use of the building. He cancelled his appearance at UMSL's What is a City Conference.

He and the author were invited to present their visions of Downtown. One showed up, the other didn't.

Bornstein and his group wanted it all. The Smithsonian would be used to eliminate the Opera House once and for all. Alan said they had not ruled out a performance or theater component, but they had already sent architects in to sketch and design the gutting of one of the world's finest large theaters.

The *Post's* Greg Freeman cited the *multi-use* capability of the Opera House. Letters pointed to its multiple-use history. The Smithsonian *idea* was floated simply as another 'excuse' or 'reason' for destroying the main theater.

July 21 1998. ULI Overlap

The ULI panel conducted interviews on *what to do with the Opera House.* The author sat with Bornstein and Baron in the Grand Hall of Union Station waiting to meet a panel member. Richard was carrying architectural drawings for Opera House re-use. The author was taking in a 32-page business plan calling for shared use.

Going to Washington

Certainly the Smithsonian would not take part in so nefarious a plan. But, I had to know. So, I flew to Washington D.C. October 9, 1999. Michael Carrigan told me the Smithsonian *never* wanted the Opera House. It had been eliminated after a walkthrough early in *1998.* I told Carrigan that is *not* what the people of St. Louis were being told. I asked him to issue a news release to the effect that the Smithsonian did not want the Opera House. He refused. I walked over to the Washington Bureau of the *Post-Dispatch*, asked National Correspondent Phil Dine to confirm the Smithsonian's position and print it in the Post so the *people* would know the truth. He did and...

October 10, 1999 The Washington Dispatch section of The Post-Dispatch confirmed with the Smithsonian's Margaret Pulles that they had pretty much ruled out the Opera House from day one. This was a $300,000 setback for Kiel Partners, Danforth and Union Station. Save face? They tried.

October 30, 1999 P-D quoted Bornstein. *Kiel was eliminated because the building was not as well suited as others to being converted to a museum.*

No, Al. It was eliminated long ago. You got caught and had to backtrack.

For museum proponents to commission drawings to *gut* a great theater indicates the level of fear and hatred of the Opera House. It didn't make sense. Nothing that is motivated by fear and greed ever makes sense. Arts killing Arts.

Lesson: In St. Louis, nothing is as it seems or as it is communicated.

It took a private citizen, on his own time and money to go to Washington D.C., call on the Smithsonian and find out what was going on and to get it before the people.

Double and Triple-Teamed

February 3, 1999, Bornstein wrote the author: The Museum Corporation is *still* considering *adaptive re-use* of Kiel Opera House, with a study of thematic and location opportunities in downtown St. Louis for one or more venues to be affiliated with the Smithsonian Institution. The author asked Bornstein to *leave the Opera House alone.*

The Fraud

Smithsonian was left *in front* of the people of St. Louis to persuade them or *condition* them that the Opera House could be sacrificed for the 'renowned' Smithsonian. It was a misrepresentation perpetuated a year-and-a-half to advance efforts to destroy Kiel. The plot was funded by Kiel Partners, the Danforth Foundation, and Union Station Partners. The *yokels* in St. Louis will believe anything. Not this time.

The media should have exposed the fraud, early on.

At UMSL's What is a City Conference in 1998 cultural experts, mostly museum people, endorsed my plan for a re-opened Kiel Opera House as a dramatic boost to the economy and cultural revitalization of downtown St. Louis. Mark Coir, director of The Cranbrook Archives in Detroit, said Mayor Harmon should talk with the mayor of Detroit about how the downtown Detroit Opera House is sparking nearby economic activity. Cleveland and Denver were cited. The Smithsonian's Stephen Weil: *performing arts are drawing the endowments.* About that time, David Darnell said we should start with *existing* resources in trying to revitalize cities and downtowns.

Kiel Opera House is a world-class cultural and economic resource. Keeping it closed to protect selfish interests tarnishes the credibility of the Downtown Now Plan, delays true economic and cultural revitalization. The

Smithsonian plan sprang from Kiel Partners' and Grand Center's *commitment* to destroy it. Kiel was a publicized *target* for more than a year after the Smithsonian itself said they were not considering it.

Smithsonian Plan will cost at least *$200 million* including seismic compliance, elaborate security, and environmental control. It would have to be subsidized. The Smithsonian brings the name, the items, stringent requirements, but no money.

Kiel Opera House can be re-opened for about $30 million, private investment, and operate profitably. There is plenty exhibit/display space.

While millions are spent to destroy Kiel Opera House, Pittsburgh opened two more theaters downtown (now has five), Cleveland re-opened its renovated Symphony Hall, and is restoring a fifth theater downtown, Seattle opened glittering Benaroya Hall, and is upgrading its opera house—$110 million.

Bookend End 2007

Smithsonian Satellite Proponents

Sauer and Miller remained in place. Laidlaw left Union Station. Bornstein joined THF. Al Kerth died. Jack Danforth said he is *through funding downtown projects and will concentrate on life sciences and biotech.*

Richard Baron opened a hotel in Cupples Station and sold it. City officials began to see the Opera House as an economic and cultural resource and tax-revenue generator. Mayor Harmon tied any further tax breaks for Kiel Center (now Savvis Center) to a re-opened Opera House. Deputy Mayor for Development Barbara Geisman told the *Post-Dispatch*: Yes we see it reopening as a *theater.* The media is reporting possible economic and cultural benefits but just are not sure who is responsible. They are concentrating more on a new ballpark, the closing of 16 public schools and major fund raising for the Symphony.

Springfield, Illinois offers the Lincoln Museum and Library and Hoagland performing arts center downtown. Kansas City restored its downtown Music Hall, expanded the World War One Museum and is building Kauffman Center for Performing Arts. Kiel Opera House with a Smithsonian presence on the lower levels would have helped St. Louis compete against these and other cities for tourism.

Kiel Opera House is still closed.

CHAPTER SEVEN

BLUES/JAZZ MUSEUM

Darlene Green, and Assistant: Steve Engelhardt
No one ever revealed a plan, ever.

Turning Kiel Opera House into a Blues/Jazz Museum was an idea promoted by comptroller Darlene Green and her assistant Steve Englehardt. It was mentioned by the ULI panel as a possibility, but it never took real shape or form. There is plenty of room in the Opera House complex for exhibits, without gutting the theater. A Clayton architect rendered a Blues/Jazz experience in one of the large theater/auditoriums for Kiel For Performing Arts.

No so-called civic leaders or City officials ever admitted Kiel Opera House has plenty of room for exhibits, without destroying the great theater.

Bookend End 2007

There never was a Plan. The idea was *floated* to destroy the Opera House main theater. It even showed up on the Downtown Now plan, for a moment. Steve Englehardt joined the Congressional Campaign staff for William "Lacy" Clay, Jr. in his successful bid to succeed his father, U.S. Congressman William Clay. There has been no further announcement of plans for a Blues/Jazz Museum. Darlene Green still holds the 'keys' to the Opera House.

The author proposed that an international Blues/Jazz festival be part of the opening week, or reopening week. Kiel Opera House always was a great place for festivals. Operating year 'round, and weather-protected, Kiel can accommodate many festivals.

Bill Kuehling, a former law partner of Harvey Harris, stonewalls Kiel at City Hall. Tom Reeves stonewalled Kiel when he was President of Downtown Now. A series of Tourism Directors have stonewalled Kiel including the current head of the SLCVC, Kitty Ratcliffe. Dick Fleming of the RCGA continues to stonewall Kiel. The Art Museum in Forest Park is raising $150 million for expansion.

Kiel Opera House is still closed.

Chapter Eight

⌖

Downtown Now Plan

1997–2000 15 Public Meetings Cost—Millions

Co-Chairs: *John Fox Arnold*, Chairman, Downtown St. Louis Partnership

Robert Baer, CEO UniGroup, Member, Civic Progress

John Danforth, Bryan Cave, St. Louis 2004

David Darnell, NationsBank,

Mike Jones, Deputy Mayor Development

Richard Fleming, RCGA and staff

Priscilla Hill-Ardoin, Southwestern Bell

John Dubinsky, Mercantile Bank

Larry Williams, Treasurer, St. Louis.

Operatives: *R. Thomas Reeves*, Executive Director, Downtown Now

Franklin D. 'Kim' Kimbrough III, President, Downtown Partnership

Phil Hoge, St. Louis Development Corporation and staff

Daniel Krasnoff, SLDC, author of ULI 'briefing' document

JoAnne LaSala, St. Louis 2004 and staff

John Hoal, Architect, Washington University, Plus Consultants, Staffs.

Progress of Decay was the challenge in the 1950s for the city of St. Louis. There were studies, reports, and plans. The Arch went up in the early '60s, a new stadium in the '70s, America's Center in the '80s, and the TWA Dome and Kiel Center in the '90s. Still, the city lost population, businesses and visitors at an alarming rate.

October 15, 1977 Mayor Harmon formed the Downtown Now Task Force 140 strong to develop a five to ten year fast-track action plan for revitalizing downtown St. Louis. Toronto's Lord Cultural Resources, was brought in to *museum* us. Zimmerman/Volk was assigned to make recommendations to re-hab. houses. St. Louis was *consultant heaven,* 1997–1999: Downtown Now, ULI, St. Louis 2004, Smithsonian studies all spent big dollars on consultants.

Downtown Now, in on the Deal

Downtown Partners *sold out* Kiel Opera House to Grand Center, before any of these studies. Downtown Partners, John Arnold quietly promised Grand Center's Ann Ruwitch the Opera House would never be part of the Downtown Now Plan.

Downtown Now operatives and consultants were told the Opera House is *not* up for discussion. To reinforce this commitment, the Chairman of Grand Center was named President of Downtown Now. For R. Tom Reeves to take the new post without dropping the former, is a conflict of interest, challenged only by the author. Reeves works for Mercantile Bank. The bank is a member of Kiel Partners Civic Progress and so forth and so on. St. Louis Development Corporation was also in on the deal—Maureen McAvey then her replacement, Phil Hoge. Dan Krasnoff did a lot of legwork on The Downtown Now project. (Krasnoff wrote the ULI study briefing document.)

Kiel was *left out* of the Downtown Now Plan, though at more than a dozen public meetings people kept bringing it up. So much for public input.

When three studies failed to *do-in* the Opera House, another hand-off was needed.

The Voice is Quicker Than the Clicker

May 27, 1999 Windows on Washington, Downtown Now held its umpteenth public meeting. This was the second at Windows. Several months before planners touted the possibility that Webster University would take over the Old Post Office. Another Downtown update listed the Convention Hotel as a done deal. Not yet.

Meetings were well attended. Downtown Partners provided refreshments. The crowd examined schematics and renderings of target area revitalization plans. Pictures were taken. Seating for 300 faced the north wall. A large screen would project visuals as the consultants presented. Round tables and working materials were prepared for small group discussion. A city official introduced consultant Joe Berich.

This meeting is to take up plans for the Gateway Mall from Union Station to Broadway. This area contains the closed Kiel Opera House and the *dead* Memorial Plaza. Recommendations to reduce traffic lanes along Market Street, add center strips and perhaps bicycle lanes would be rejected by Mayor Clarence Harmon.

The Opera House had not been rendered on any drawings or graphics by Downtown Now, up until tonight. What might change that. Opera House is in the *critical mass* area, the geographic area to be covered in the meeting.

Three Dots

Fifteen minutes in Berich projected a visual with three dots plotted on an outline of Kiel Opera House. (I don't remember if they were red or white, but they were there, on the screen). Without breaking stride, Joe said the Opera House was one of three possible locations for a Smithsonian satellite in downtown St. Louis. This was more than a year *after* the Smithsonian had eliminated the Opera House for consideration. The St. Louis Museum Group was still publicizing Kiel as a possible location.

Before Joe changed the visual, the author rose and asked *would it not be criminal to use one cultural institution to destroy another,* to use the Smithsonian to destroy Kiel Opera House? *There is plenty of room for exhibits, without destroying the theater.* There was a smattering of applause. Berich agreed: *That is not the intent.* Then he went on.

What was really going on here? As in: *really.* Urban Land Institute *didn't get it done.* They handed it off to the 2004 Cultural Study, which *didn't get it done.* 2004 handed it off to the Smithsonian Satellite study. They *didn't get it done.* So, they handed it off to Downtown Now. They didn't get it done. Were the handoffs covered in the media? No. Did the three dots ever appear on another Downtown Now visual? No.

ST. LOUIS, MO. FOR IMMEDIATE RELEASE 10/19/99

Stating that *the Grand Center/Fox Theater stranglehold* on Kiel Opera House must finally be forced open, Ed Golterman, K-FPA Chairman, calls for the resignation of Thomas Reeves as the new head of Downtown Now. "As President of Grand Center, Reeves defines conflict of interest. He can not protect the Fox and revitalize downtown St. Louis, culturally", said Golterman. "Grand Center has vigorously and consistently opposed re-opening Kiel Opera House for more nearly a decade", said Golterman. That has not helped bring downtown back. K-FPC, Inc. will hold open board meetings every Monday evening at six PM at Talayna's (on Debaliviere two blocks north of Lindell).

K-FPA is also planning vigils in front of the Opera House on Halloween, Thanksgiving and New Year's, to honor *a civic resource that has been so dishonored.*

Action Reeves pledged to take action. Reeves continued to hold the conflicting roles, Reeves, Fleming, Eagleton and Danforth were turned down by the Missouri Legislature for more tax money for infrastructure work in downtown St. Louis.

Trust in downtown plans continues to erode, even in Jefferson City. Perhaps the answers are not in Jefferson City, or in City Hall but in keeping a promise. It probably did not help the Downtown Now proponents in Jefferson City, that both the Blues and Cardinals were knocking on legislators' doors for tax help. The answer was the same, for all, at least in this session—*No.*

Bookend End 2007

Kim Kimbrough was replaced by Jim Cloar at Downtown Partnership. Cloar came from Tampa (*where they have a proud tradition of building public boondoggle and tearing down things*—RFT). He promotes whatever he is told to promote. The Old Post Office reopened. It holds mostly non-revenue producing tenants. The project was heavily subsidized by the public. The Art Museum wants to take more space in Forest Park and wouldn't consider a satellite in The Post Office.

John Fox Arnold protects Grand Center. He organized a third fund raiser for Mayor Clarence Harmon. Harmon lost to Aldermanic President Francis Slay. Vince Schoemehl then held a fund raiser for Slay in Grand Center. Danforth protects Grand Center. Tom Reeves protects Grand Center. David

Darnell protects Grand Center. Is there a credibility problem here boys, a little lack of trust? You do not operate in a vacuum. People are looking closely. The *fix* is still in.

Would people not trust downtown projects more, had they kept one promise? Could not naming/sponsorship revenue from the Opera House help the Symphony: Arts helping Arts instead of Arts killing Arts? Keeping Kiel Opera House off the table, or bastardizing it into something else is dishonorable. The vultures continue to circle but people are watching, in St. Louis City, St. Louis County and Jefferson City.

The Cardinals built and opened their new ballpark in record time and won the 2006 World Series. the City is negotiating a changed or expanded Ballpark Village plan but 2007 ends with a huge hole in the ground and the Village will not be ready for the 2009 All Star Game. The Blues and Scottrade Center operate in a dead zone. Renaissance Grand could not make loan interest payments for three years.

Kiel Opera House is still closed

CHAPTER NINE

TURN IT INTO A SCHOOL

FOX THEATER OWNER HARVEY HARRIS AND COMMITTEE FOR THE SCHOOL FOR PERFORMING ARTS

November, 2002, Fox Theater owner Harvey Harris and Alberici Construction's Bob McCoole brought before the School Board a plan to re-configure the Opera House into a school for performing arts. The project would cost about $75 million, funded primarily through tax money and tax credits, including $25 million in desegregation settlement money. (Kiel Opera House was always *desegregated,* it served all.)

Blues President Sauer was quoted in the Post: *The Lauries would be willing to help.* Sure it included workout facilities for their hockey players. School Board President Bill Purdy asked Harris and his group to provide a specific proposal. Harris expanded his committee to include Urban League President James Buford, and at least two members of the Black Leadership Roundtable. The author alerted Superintendent Cleveland Hammonds and the Board this was an obvious attempt to use the schools as a *vehicle* for finishing off Kiel.

The Post carried my assessment of what was really going on; Jeff Rainford of the Mayor's Office denied it. But it was *out there.* They simply *could not proceed.* Hammonds said he felt a school for performing arts should be closer to Grand Avenue. The Board agreed and declined participation in the Harris plan.

Hammonds resigned. A slate of candidates led by Grand Center President Vince Schoemehl took control of the schools for three years. Harris then grabbed a *piece* of Don Breckenridge's deal to re-open Kiel Opera House, announced a few days before a 1993 School Board meeting.

Bookend End 2007

The St. Louis School Board has dealt with massive problems over the years.

It did not need to get involved in killing Kiel Opera House. But, without missing a step, Harris weaseled his way into the Breckenridge deal.

Kiel Opera House is still closed.

Chapter Ten

Breckenridge, Harris, Abrams

Another Non-deal

Monday, May 6, 2003, Developer Don Breckenridge announced plans to restore and reopen Kiel Opera House. (The author had asked Breckenridge to help since 1998, and had shared business plans with him). Martinez and Johnson would be the theater architects. They said: *the Opera House was in great shape.*

At the eleventh hour (as the media put it), Fox Theater owner Harvey Harris *weaseled* his way into the deal (as I put it). The Fox and Clear Channel would share bookings. All Kiel ever needed from Harris was to *leave it alone.* Clear Channel made St. Louis wait in line while it developed and opened other theaters around the country, including Boston Opera House. Blue's President Mark Sauer said there will be no Opera House without more parking and that was echoed by Clear Channel. Breckenridge looked nervous.

From day one, the announcement in the Opera House foyer at an invitation-only event, this stunk as sharply as the urine and vomit stains that cover the 14th Street entrances. A Breckenridge spokesperson to Riverfront Times: *Ed has been a good advocate for Kiel, but will have no official role in the project.*

The deal collapsed over an unnecessary dispute over The Abrams Building. Rev. Larry Rice wanted it as a center for the homeless. The City presumably wants it for parking and support services for Kiel. All Mayor Slay had to do was offer Rice another downtown building. Instead, Rainford and Breckenridge and Dan Buck, President of St. Patrick's Center, verbally attacked Rice. The Abrams battle went to court.

Bookend End 2007

Don Breckenridge died November 30, 2005. In 2006, Minneapolis opened the new Guthrie Theater and expanded a museum, downtown. Nashville opened a $147 million Symphony Hall and still offers Tennessee Center for Performing Arts. Madison, Wisconsin added another theater to Overture Center. Kansas City reopened its restored Music Hall this year and will open Kauffman Center for Performing Arts in 2010. Layers of corruption and dirty deals stonewall Kiel at a time she is most needed.

Kiel Opera House is still closed.

CHAPTER ELEVEN

THE MEDIA

WHERE'S DON MARSH WHEN YOU NEED HIM?

If Civic Progress *blessed* destruction of The Ambassador Theater, Kiel Auditorium, and The Arena, and the closing, damaging and wasting of Kiel Opera House, a compliant media *rolled over*. They made a little noise but didn't challenge.

The media *must* do more than cover *hot* issues. The damage is usually done when there *seems* to be nothing going on. Damage is done behind closed doors. This is when St. Louis needs a probing, investigating media.

In Chapter 4, the ULI Study, we identified *patterns* in media coverage. These patterns are somewhat understandable, not unlike other cities. The difference is there seems to be a shortage of investigative reporting *before* the damage is done, and a lot of lamenting, *afterward*. The coverage, or lack thereof, of Civic Progress' control over St. Louis bears at least short treatment. Is the media at least partially responsible for leaving citizens and taxpayers vulnerable to this control?

It's a mixed bag. Reporters and editorial writers want to *dig into* the players and the *plays*. Economically, *The Post, St. Louis Business Journal* and perhaps some radio and TV stations are heavily dependent upon Civic Progress and member companies for advertising revenue. KMOX radio used to do editorials but not any more. The Post calls its editorials—Opinions. Investigative reporting is usually after-the-fact and seldom calls for formal investigations. Few push for observing and enforcing Sunshine Laws.

The Spinners

Civic Progress and many of its member companies enjoy the services of Fleishman-Hillard, founded and headquartered in St. Louis. These word-and-image-makers *advance* Civic Progress' goals by disseminating information. They are also master stonewallers, shielding their clients from media probes. F-H *works* The *Post-Dispatch* hard on behalf of its clients. The *Post* rubber stamps most of the Civic Progress agenda for example: the replacement ballpark and Ballpark Village.

Just as the City was reluctant to challenge Kiel Partners to make good on their promise to re-open the Opera House, the media has been reluctant to shake the cages. With The Downtown Now Plan and a series of related or unrelated studies it was hard to keep Kiel Opera House buried. To her credit, Comptroller Green said we just can not ignore it, and undertook the ULI Study. This was an opening, a slight opening.

Newspaper Editorials on Kiel Opera House

- *St. Louis Business Journal*, March 2, 1998.
  Raise the Curtain on the Kiel Opera House Is another study needed?

- *St. Louis Post-Dispatch,* July, 1998
  Will UMSL trump Kiel? Chancellor Blanche Touhill has always said UMSL's facility is not a rival to a renovated Kiel Opera House. Many cities use performing arts centers to rejuvenate their downtowns. We should think twice before we abandon that idea here.

- *St. Louis Post-Dispatch,* August 16, 1998
  A Promise is a Promise. Nothing has altered Kiel Partners' obligation to refurbish Kiel. The (ULI) task force produced research that is fundamentally flawed, including basic factorial errors about how many theaters there are and how many seats they offer.

- *St. Louis Post-Dispatch*, September 1998
  A Deal is a Deal. The money to refurbish the building—no matter what its ultimate use—must come from Kiel Partners. To forget that original agreement, even if it seems pragmatic in the short run, is to set an intolerable precedent.

- *St. Louis Post-Dispatch*, October 1998
  The Kiel Opera House is in legal and governmental limbo and its fate may be sealed by teams of consultants, rather than by the people of St. Louis.

- *St. Louis Post-Dispatch, December 13, 1998*
  Arts and Culture. The disappointing aspects of this study (2004 cultural study) is the absence of ideas for downtown and the discounting of the Kiel Opera House. Reviving Kiel Opera House could be a powerful catalyst to the revival of downtown.

- *St. Louis Post-Dispatch* January 22, 1999
  The presumptuous Mr. Sauer. Kiel Center lies at the end of a trail of civic chaos. Two historic buildings (Opera House and The Arena) have had the life squeezed out of them. One is in imminent danger of demolition, because of Kiel Partners. When it comes to reopening Kiel Opera House, Kiel Partners should simply write a check.

- *St. Louis Jewish Light*, June 1999
  Lois Caplan *Raise Kiel's Curtain*. Reprinted in Intermission July–August 1999. Very good acoustically and the sight lines were excellent—a perfect venue for opera, plays, ballets and festivals.

- *St. Louis Post-Dispatch*, September 9, 1999
  Save Kiel Opera House. A restored Opera House, especially as a performance space, would add to the region's cultural mix. Bill Laurie says they'd have to get a feel from the community, would be willing to listen.

- *St. Louis Post-Dispatch*, February 2, 2000
  Lessons in Leadership
  The biggest challenge facing the arts community is to ensure that UMSL's (Blanche Touhill) success doesn't lead to unintended consequences: dismissing any future for Kiel Opera House and neglecting the needs of small and mid-size performing arts companies that are desperate for space.

- *St. Louis County Journals*, August 8, 1999
  Restore Kiel as a place for music. The building's beauty, history and ideal location in a downtown that desperately needs to attract more visitors and revenue demands a restoration to its glory years, for performances. Put museums, elsewhere.

- *St. Louis Journalism Review*, September 1999
  Civic Progress vetoes ideas and proposals of those who are not sufficiently obsequious to the powers that be. The latest example is its opposition to the reopening of one of the most architecturally significant performing arts centers ever built in the United States, Kiel Opera House.

- *Post-Dispatch* Columnist Greg Freeman has called for decision-makers to keep an open mind, cited Kiel's multiple-use capability and asked the Lauries to listen to Mr. Golterman, and his group. Freeman appeared with the author on the St. Louis cable channel special on the Opera House, and hosted a show on the public radio station UMSL, with the author and H. Russell Carter.

- Letters to Editors flooded newspapers. Dozens were printed including 15 in the Post's *Imagine St. Louis* section, November 14, 1999.

- *Riverfront Times* described most studies on Kiel as biased. Publisher Ray Hartmann frequently put Civic Progress' or City Hall's feet to the fire. D. J. Wilson wrote articles on the ULI Study, the 2004 Cultural Study and Downtown Now. *Riverfront Times nailed* Kiel Partners/Civic Progress, time and time again for not keeping their contractual promise to re-open the Opera House.

- *Intermission Magazine and St. Louis Core climbed on* the Opera House issue and let hardly an issue go by without a story. The St. Louis Times did a nice feature as did the Webster-Kirkwood Times.

- *Il Pensiero*, the Italian Community Newspaper, has been supportive of Kiel.

Radio and TV coverage increased markedly. Citizens began calling *talk shows.*

Channel 30's Don Marsh delivered the most thorough TV report—reminding viewers of Kiel Partners' promise. He reported on the fear of City officials to go against Civic Progress. And, he reported on our efforts to break the logjam on Kiel.

The media generally depends on the people to launch and keep such efforts going. Those trying to effect real change in St. Louis are not looking for coverage, they are looking to make positive change, and to the media for help.

Could not one reporter spot the self-interests being served by these *studies*—beforehand?

Could not one publication, columnist, radio or TV station call for investigations into violation of civil and criminal law? The media walks up to the edge of the water, dips its toe in, but then *pulls back*.

Why did a private citizen have to go to Washington D.C. to uncover the Smithsonian fraud and bring it before the people? How heavily would a Smithsonian presence in St. Louis have to be subsidized? Do advertising dollars and strong-arm tactics control the media on certain issues?

The St. Louis media did not protect the citizens during the 1990s from destruction of civic or historic buildings. Perhaps they will do so in the new millennium.

Turnover in street reporters covering four to five stories a day makes it difficult for stations to do in-depth investigative reporting. They do quick exposes then, on to the next story.

On June 26th, 2000 Pulitzer Publishing announced it would purchase The Suburban Journals and The Ladue News. This would merge the region's two largest circulation newspaper operations. A monopoly becomes a mega-monopoly. P-D management: *news and editorial departments will operate independently.*

Don Corrigan in Webster-Kirkwood Times doubted that important questions would be fully discussed in the P-D. He writes *The Justice Department seldom challenges media mergers, despite their responsibilities to uphold the law and fight monopolies.*

The media's protective cloak around Civic Progress, Kiel Center and Grand Center just got thicker and warmer. The merger has not been formally challenged as possibly violating anti-trust legislation. Keeping Kiel closed has not seriously been challenged.

Coverage of the Arts in St. Louis centers on the Symphony's plight, Stages leaving Kirkwood and building and expanding museums. Kiel Opera House could help the Symphony and Stages, and house traveling or permanent art exhibits.

Under the *Post's* Nearly Exclusive Watch

Since the *Globe-Democrat* closed and the Post emerged as the major daily in St. Louis Kiel Convention Hall was destroyed, the Opera House—damaged and looted, the Ambassador Theater and the Arena—destroyed. What

will be the next unchallenged destruction? Will the people have any protective voice? Who will do the investigations or call for investigations? Radio
and TV stations could once again editorialize. But, they would have to be
free from pressure from advertisers.

Prepared for *St. Louis Journalism Review,* April 15, 2000: *Finishing The Play* (excerpts) Ed L. Golterman

In basketball, finishing the play is a slam-dunk off a rebound, fast break
and two passes. In baseball, the catcher tagging out the runner on a relay to
the plate is finishing the play. In hockey it is a deflection in front of the net.

In downtown St. Louis, *finishing the play* will be the final destruction
of Kiel Opera House following years of fouls, penalties, errors, double and
triple-teaming that have never been *called*. In downtown St. Louis the *referee*,
the *Post-Dispatch*, looks on silently with the whistle tugged in its shirt and
the flag nestled in its back pocket.

When the Cole Campbell era is chronicled it will be identified as the
time investigative reporting about died at the Post in favor of *feel good, send
us your letters* journalism.

Jerry Berger and Joan Dames *taught* the P-D that folks like to see their
names in print (most of the time). Letters, commentaries and *imaginings*
imply public participation.

While people enjoy the recognition, Civic Progress strengthens control
on major decisions including those that have brought the Downtown Now
Plan and the Stadium plan to a points-of-distrust. Fool me once, fool me
twice, but not three times.

Kiel Opera House—one of the finest large theaters in the world—is kept
closed in a downtown that is nearly void of year 'round entertainment.

P-D: Get in the Game or Throw the Flag

Post-Dispatch columnists have referred to the Opera House as an asset
with potential but The Paper is still at water's edge. Ellen Futterman called for
another study on the Kiel Opera House. That would be the fifth, or sixth.

Cleveland offers five theaters and a symphony hall pouring people and
money into downtown Cleveland. St. Louis never needed the first *study*. The
media has had all the information it has needed to take a decisive stance.
There is nothing more to learn. There are no more studies to do. Not decid-

ing is deciding. Print vigorous editorials for its restoration and re-opening of Kiel Opera House with private funding from those responsible, or call for investigations.

Investigate every instance in which special interests override public good. Direct the attention of responsible agencies toward investigations. It should not be the responsibility of citizens to protect their own interests. It is the responsibility of the media, of elected and appointed officials, and of law enforcement agencies to protect the public's interests.

The *Post-Dispatch* should have started blowing the whistle and *throwing the flag* long ago, against the players and the plays. It should have *thrown* the flag in 1992 at those who signed the lease that destroyed The Kiel Convention Hall, damaged and looted the Opera House and restricted The Arena to non-admission events.

If *finishing the play* in downtown St. Louis means the final destruction of the Kiel Opera House will anything proposed for Downtown St. Louis ever be believed?

If *finishing the play* means keeping a promise, who knows how exciting the revitalization of downtown St. Louis really can be. Does The Media have a role and a responsibility?

Tell us what other cities are really doing, and that we can do it too.

May 3, 2000

Mr. Terrence Egger – Publisher
St. Louis Post-Dispatch,
900 N. Tucker
St. Louis, MO 63101

Dear Terry,

The continued *sacrificing* of Kiel Opera House to protect Grand Center is the issue that has destroyed trust in The Downtown Now Plan. The greedy attempted money grabs by the Cardinals and the Blues also destroys that trust.

Until the dishonor of the Opera House ends, the Blues will never get out of the first round. They perform in a dishonorable building, created through damage and deceit. The Post has a chance to help *course-correct*. The way to course-correct this is to publish my business plan, call for *naming* money for restoring, re-opening the Opera House and get it away from the sports thugs, finally. Or, you can conclude that we need more museums and a new stadium.

Are you really going to report the RCGA and Sports Commission studies and *recommendations* on a new stadium as independent and believable? There has not been an independent study of anything in St. Louis.

Ed L. Golterman

Kiel Opera House faded out of the news. The author walked to Columbia, Missouri. to find out what Bill Laurie was going to do with it. This generated statewide coverage. Whatever is going on with Kiel is going on behind closed doors.

P-D's editors told the author; we *won't run anything on the Opera House until something happens to it.* In other words—we will not investigate (March 2001).

Bookend End 2007

Blues' owner Bill Laurie wasted Kiel Opera House for five years. The City should take the lease and re-open it to end this waste, Opera House advocate Ed Golterman.

Laurie has never *been open to re-opening the Opera House, and the city should never have given him control,* he added.

Since 1998, the author has submitted multiple business-marketing plans for operation of the Opera House as a multi-venue performance, cultural and events center. Financing would be primarily through private funding. 900,000 a year could be drawn to Kiel from throughout the region and the mid west—generating jobs, income, benefits and four to five million a year in tax revenue.

In February, 2000. Kiel Opera House was given National Historic Place status through efforts of Ed Golterman, Kiel for Performing Arts, and Landmarks Association. The City will not honor Kiel with its historic plaque. *There's a plaque on nearly every old building downtown except the one that deserves it the most*)

November 4, 2002, the City *cut* a ballpark deal. The next day, the voters approved a charter amendment giving them a vote before any public assistance could be given to the Cardinals owners. They were a day too late.

Fourth Quarter of 2002, Harvey Harris, an owner of the Fox Theater, proposes to gut the Opera House and turn it into a school for performing arts.

Sunday, December 8, 2002 *Post-Dispatch*. Buried at the bottom of Jerry Berger's column: *Clear Channel is apparently bowing out of its offer to re-open Kiel Opera* House.

Is the media bought off or scared off, or both? There was sparse coverage of the Breckenridge deal and it didn't happen. There has been sparse coverage of the Checketts deal. These deals remain behind closed doors.

Kiel Opera House is still closed.

Chapter Twelve

Civic Progress, Or Regress

April 7, 2000

St. Louis *Post-Dispatch*
Commentary by Dave Drebes,
Former President of Metropolis St. Louis.
(*partial*)

"Any community should be so blessed with the passionate, but once they upset The Order of Things, they are suddenly not to be taken seriously. Remember? Bob Cassilly shows up with a check and dream for The Arena and he goes from creative genius to *kook*. Ed Golterman shows too much persistence about Kiel Opera House and he goes from passionate believer to *kook*. Who will be kookified this year—Joe Edwards for daring to develop further east on Delmar? Bert Walker for pushing Home Rule? Or may be it will be Eddie Roth for trying to make the zoning code more *nuns* friendly".

Ed Golterman to Dick Liddy Civic Progress Chairman, April 1998:
You listen to the wrong *advisers.*
Dick to Ed: Thanks for your candor.
Ed to Dick: July 2000: You still listen to the wrong advisors.

Civic Progress IS Kiel Partners IS Clark Enterprises IS Downtown Now IS 2004 IS the RCGA IS Grand Center IS Forest Park Forever. Following were Civic Progress Members and Companies at the time of the Kiel deals 1990–1992.

Kiel Center Partners	Civic Progress
Ameren UE (formerly Union Electric)	Charles W. Mueller
Anheuser-Busch Cos.	August A. Busch III
Commerce Bancshares Inc.	David W. Kemper
Edison Brothers Stores	Alan Miller
Emerson Electric	Charles F. Knight
Enterprise Rent-A-Car	Andrew Taylor
General American Life Insurance	Richard A. Liddy
Laclede Gas Co.	Robert C. Jaudes
Mallickrodt Inc.	C. Ray Holman
Maritz Inc	William E. Maritz
The May Department Stores	David C. Farrell
Mercantile Bank Corp.	Thomas H. Jacobsen
Monsanto Company	Robert B. Shapiro
NationsBank (Later Bank of America)	Andrew B. Craig III
Ralston Purina	William P. Stiritz
Schnucks Markets. Inc	Craig D. Schnuck
Southwestern Bell Telephone	Edward A Mueller
Sverdrup Corporation	Richard Buemer

Members who declined to participate directly in the Kiel Center deal have been spared more than $50 million in *keep-us-going* money: A.G. Edwards–Benjamin F. Edwards III; Brown Groups–B. A. Bridgwater; Furniture Brands Int.–Richard B. Loynd; Harbour Groups' Sam Fox; Jefferson Smurfit–James E. Terrill; Edward Jones; McDonnell Douglas–Harry C. Stonecipher; UniGroup–Robert J. Baer; Venture Stores, Inc.–Robert Wildrick; Wettereau–Ted C. Wettereau.

Civic Progress–Collaborators, *agents-operatives:*

- Bryan Cave Law Firm. Walter Metcalfe signed the Kiel Center lease of 1991.

- Lashy and Baer Law Firm–John Fox Arnold.

- Fleishman-Hillard–Public Relations Council Primary consultant, Al Kerth III, Sr. Partner, signed 1991 Kiel Partners Lease. Kerth was a member of ULI Task Force and the Smithsonian Satellite Project.

- General American Life's Former CEO, and former member of Civic Progress, Edwin S. Trusheim. Trusheim signed the 1991 Kiel Partners Lease. Liddy replaced him on C-P.

- John Bachmann is Chairman of the Board, St. Louis Symphony (Grand Center).

- David Farrell, May Companies; banker Tom Jacobsen and Trusheim are Symphony

- Life Trustees. Commerce Bank's David Kemper; Emerson's Chuck Knight; Liddy; and Jack Taylor, Enterprise Leasing; are on the Board of Trustees.

- Board of Directors of Opera Theater of Webster Groves includes: Mrs. B.A. Bridgwater, Jr. David Darnell, NationsBank now Bank of America (later replaced Craig on Civic Progress, Kiel Partners): Richard Liddy, Piscilla Hill-Ardoin, Southwestern Bell.

Far-Reaching Control

Civic Progress controls the major projects and decisions that affect St. Louis and its residents. This power extends deeply into City Hall. It works its *will*, at will.

Its *will* is also worked through memberships on each others boards, on boards of other corporations, foundations and civic and cultural agencies. If Civic Progress says Kiel Opera House will not *compete* with the Fox Theater, it is so.

More serious than just wielding power and control, is its closed-mindedness. Since it closed Kiel, 200 cities and towns have restored and reopened downtown performing arts centers or built new ones. They have been unable to keep or draw corporate headquarters to St. Louis. They keep Kiel Center and the Blues afloat but will not complete that building to generate more jobs, income, revenue and traffic.

Civic Progress Downtown *Achievements* in the 1990s: TWA Dome, Kiel Center.

Early 2000s—Old Post Office, a convention hotel, a new ballpark and a casino. While the sports *gods* are adored, businesses, industries and people continue to vacate the City.

In the cultural and entertainment fields, Civic Progress has allowed downtown St. Louis to pretty much die: Destruction of Kiel Auditorium, closing Kiel Opera House, destruction of the Ambassador Theater, modifying the American Theater so it can't present book shows, and *shelving* ideas or proposals that do not *come out* of Civic Progress or obtain its blessing.

The Media And Civic Progress–Friendly Sparing

Columnists poke *fun* at Civic Progress—old white guys, out of touch—holding closed meetings at exclusive clubs. But, the media seldom goes much deeper. The media does not challenge the *substance* of what Civic Progress plans, authorizes, directs or funds, before the fact. Media, and citizens *lament* decisions and actions after the fact.

Fear of Civic Progress is real and widespread. In trying to re-open the Opera House, we encountered business people, arts people, people in entertainment and in the media who *feared* the big boys. *Good luck, I'd like to help, but I can't. Here's a contribution but don't use my name. I can't help. I have a conflict of interest. Are THEY going to let you do this?*

Since early 1998, I have sent copies of the business/use plan to leading members of Civic Progress, particularly to the *new* members, hoping a leader would emerge. I had hoped the Taylors, or Barry Beracha, or Bob Baer would step forward. And, of course I tried with August Busch and Chuck Knight. Please *Course-Correct*.

Downtown cannot come back on sports venues and casinos alone. Past promises—to the Fox, to UMSL, perhaps now to SLU—cannot continue to rule. It is more important to attend to Downtown than to protect existing or planned entities. You have the power to sacrifice Kiel Opera House. You do not have the right. True leaders course-correct.

Bookend End 2007

Civic Progress remains silent on Kiel Opera House. They are out from under their Kiel Center debts and *problems*. They refuse to go back in and *make it right*.

Kiel Opera House is still closed.

CHAPTER THIRTEEN

OPEN YOUR MINDS

Following are from 52 of 300 letters and e-mails. These are separate from letters to editors and 4,700 who signed petitions. These are from people who took time to express support mostly by snail mail.

"It has a value that transcends the marketplace. Somehow our predecessors who built the Kiel understood this in ways that now escape us."

Bob Archibald, Historian

"My personal belief is that we are crazy to let such a beautiful structure deteriorate any further."

Dave Benson, Television Producer

"A truly beautiful and big building that could be a real asset to St. Louis and downtown."

Jane Buri

"I wish you well in your battle to get Kiel Opera House re-opened. I'm always glad to hear of such enthusiastic support for our arts."

Baritone Philip Burke

"Such a magnificent building deserves to be used on a regular basis to be enjoyed by everyone in the region."

Leslie Cantu, St. Louis Resident

"God Bless, and Keep Up the Good Work. A Museum, indeed."

Joan Caro, St. Louis

"This magnificent building should once again fulfill its civic role as a place of the people, as soon as possible."

Hon. William L. Clay, U.S. Congressman, Missouri's 1st District

"Right on target with downtown revitalization. Your mayor should talk with the mayor of Detroit."

Mark Coir, Cranbrook Archives

"Now that Kiel is on its way to be a historically-recognized building, is there any chance of getting back some of the items that disappeared during its days in limbo."

Julie Edison, Washington, D.C.

"Let's not miss the opportunity to preserve Kiel Opera House for our city, for our children and for our future."

Bill Federer, Author/Businessman

"In addition to the economic and cultural benefits of retaining Kiel as it was meant to be, I believe preserving such hallmarks is the tradition of our past and will secure the vision of our city's future."

Richard Frain, Financial Services

"We support the rehab and would be interested in use of an assembly hall."

Fran Friedman, President, Broadway Fantasies

"Keep going strong with the Opera House—make it a juicy opportunity for everyone—especially the opposition."

John Golterman, Composer/Performer, New York

"I want to hear voices and music ring through the beautiful interior of Kiel, again."

Jennifer Grotpeter, Granddaughter of Kiel Architect

"Best wishes in your worthy endeavor."

Tom Guilfoil, Attorney

"Jane and I have always been firmly of the view that Kiel Opera House should be retained as the City's primary performing arts facility."

Whitney Harris

"The St. Louis Opera Guild would applaud any effort to develop additional performance space in St. Louis, especially space that would be conducive to opera performances."

Mary Huber, President, St. Louis Opera Guild

"Thank you for your leadership in the revitalization of downtown St. Louis through the potential renovation, refurbishment and reopening of Kiel Opera House."

John Hylton, Chairman, Music Department, University of Missouri–St. Louis

"You have our permission to use the Kiel family name in your efforts with the Kiel Opera House. Thank you for your generous efforts to do that."

Paul J. Kiel

"Kiel Opera House should be the major cultural attraction along the Gateway Mall, that is Market Street."

Michael Kiesler, St. Louis County

"I would be delighted to act as a consultant or in any other capacity in which you feel I might be helpful."

John Kinnamon, President, Burn Brae Dinner Theater

"Bringing alive Kiel as a center for the arts will infuse the City with a commitment to offer balance to the experiences of our residents."

Chris Limber, Producer

"For the Italian community, music has always been our joy, or heritage and inspiration, and Kiel Opera House, is a place we valued for its beauty and performances."

Antonino e Lina Lombardo, publishers, Il Pensiero

"I will surly do what I can."

Joseph B McGlynn, Jr., Attorney at Law, Chairman, St. Patrick's Day Parade

"Reunifying the City and County and Re-Opening Kiel are two dreams that are very worthy."

Bill Maritz, Civic and Business Leader

"All the best to you in your efforts to save Kiel Opera House."

Josie McDonald, Springboard for Learning and Mid-Sized Arts Cooperative

"Like many, I have wonderful memories of the Kiel Opera House. We need this venue restored."

Patricia Morrissey, St. Louis

"The Opera House must be save and utilized."

Robert Nelson, St. Louis

"We here at Lyric Opera of Chicago, can only wish you well in your efforts to re-open the Kiel Opera House."

Danny Newman. Public Relations Counsel

OPEN YOUR MINDS

"The Opera House will open in 1995."

Judd Perkins, President, Kiel Center

"A viable Kiel Opera House would result in more activity for surrounding businesses, resulting in more taxes for the City."

Gary Pohrer, Downtown Business Operator

"Your efforts are much appreciated by many people in this City."

Joseph Ragni, Media Executive

"Kiel Opera House renovation is a necessary step in bringing residents and visitors together with music, dance, exhibits and special events."

8th Ward Alderman Lewis Reed

"Wishing you much success in reviving Kiel Opera House."

Marianne Stanek, Retired, Monsanto

"Your involvement (to Jeff Stewart) with Kiel Opera House sounds great. Please let me know what I can do to help."

Alan Sues, Performer/Producer

"We are supportive of your efforts to have the Kiel Opera House restored and made available for arts groups. The Restored Allen Theater in Cleveland is expected to draw 300,000 a year."

Harry F. Swanger, Executive Director, Compton Heights Concert Band

"I believe the city needs a 'grand' opera house, for many purposes. It would bring the people together and create a thriving metropolitan area."

Fern Rosen, Talent Agent

"Think big, think beyond our own backyard. Cleveland, Pittsburgh, Seattle, Detroit, Nashville and San Francisco all have multiple performing arts centers, all of which are thriving and rejuvenating their downtown."

Bruce C. Ward, Financial Services

"There are a lot of people who want to get behind what you are doing."

Rick Hunter, Metropolis

"Let me know what I can do to help."

Charles Hefti, Producer

"Good luck with your Opera House Honor Guard."

Viviane Picard, Soprano

"It is a world-class facility. If done right it will have an enormously positive impact on downtown St. Louis."

Ray Shepardson, GSI Architects, Cleveland

"I too would like to see it used for performances arts here in St. Louis."

Aldermanic President Francis Slay

"I certainly support you efforts to re-open Kiel Opera House. Opera should belong to people in venues for presentation that all can afford to attend."

Tenor Hugh Smith

"It just needs marketing."

Bruce Sommer, America's Center

"Your generation has given us a lot to fix, but also a lot to build upon."

Matt Stevens, Metropolis

"I think it takes an entertainer like yourself to appreciate the true beauty of the building. I'm glad you're working on it."

Author-columnist Elaine Viets

"We would welcome the refurbishing and opening of Kiel Opera House and would love nothing more than to be able to call it Our Home, Too."

Marilyn B. Wibbenmeyer-Stanza, President, Ballet Company

"I write to support your work to renovate and restore Kiel Opera House and its *attendant* spaces. I see other cities successfully using performing spaces for urban renewal."

Agnes Wilcox, The New Theater

"The re-opening of the Opera House will offer another excellent venue for the many people who love and support the arts, performers and audiences alike."

David C. Williams, Band Dir., Berkeley Middle School

"Theaters and performing arts centers are *drawing the endowments*."

Stephen Weil, Emeritus Senior Scholar, Smithsonian Institution

"The Kiel building should be one of the centerpieces of the Downtown area. I am shocked that the current planning does not include that beautiful place which most cities would give their 'eye teeth' to have."

Jack Walters, M.D.

St. Louis Board of Aldermen Resolution 125, July 1, 1999

WHEREAS, throughout the nation. The performing arts and their attendant facilities are playing a vital role in rejuvenating the nation's downtown areas, attracting citizens downtown and fostering increased traffic and activity, and

WHEREAS, the Kiel Opera House has the potential to once again become such a facility within the City of St. Louis, and

WHEREAS, the Kiel Opera House could become a world class music hall as well as additional exhibit spaces, and has the capacity sufficient to host several simultaneous events; and

WHEREAS, these features could enable it to be a key factor in bringing people back to our region's core for business and recreation; and

WHEREAS, opening this complex once again as a civic, music, dance, drama, festival, cultural and special events exhibits center would augment downtown revitalization efforts currently underway, and is supported by organizations such as the Missouri Chapter of the International Special Events Society, and

WHEREAS, the City will receive many benefits, both economic and social, as a result of this increased activity, including jobs, increased revenue, and an improved perception of downtown among the citizens of the region, that will foster further investment and growth,

BE IT THEREFORE RESOLVED that The St. Louis Board of Aldermen expresses its interest in the continued consideration of all possible alternatives and combined uses for utilization of the Kiel Opera House facility, including its use as a venue for the performing arts, to serve as a catalyst for increased downtown vitality.

Introduced on this the 1st day of July, 1999, by: Alderman Lewis Reed and Board President Francis Slay Adopted on this the 1st day of July, 1999, as attested by:

Fred F. Steffen
Clerk, Board of Aldermen

Francis G. Slay
President, Board of Aldermen

Bookend End 2007

Civic Progress: Closed Minds, Closed Doors, Closed Check Books. But, massive flows of money go to save Symphony, to pave over Forest Park, for

The Zoo, Science Center, Botanical Gardens, Museums. Most are *day-time* attractions—in and out.

September 18, 2002. Enterprise announced a $30 million grant to the Botanical Gardens to study and categorize plants in South America.

In 2007 Gateway Foundation committed $25 million for more dead art on the Gateway Mall east of Tucker (12th Street.) The Memorial Plaza west of Tucker remains a deadzone.

The Museum people are close to raising $150 million to expand the Art Museum (In a city without a downtown performing arts center).

Kiel Opera House can draw 800,000 a year—New Business. Growth. Look downtown.

Kiel Opera House is still closed.

Chapter Fourteen

Advised and Warned

Kiel opera house (KMOX Radio, from Cleveland)
Friday, August 20, 1999. Charlie Brennan and Carol Daniel–Hosts Paul
Westlake, Jr. FAIA–Guest. Commissioner of Architecture, U.S. Institute
of Theater Technology, and Partner-van Dijk, Pace and Westlake.

His firm designed the plan for the theaters in Playhouse Square;
Denver Performing Arts Center; Orpheum Theater in Phoenix;
and others. The author took Westlake's partner, Peter van Dijk,
through the Opera House in July of 1999. (Brennan is in The Rock and Roll
Museum, with Westlake. Daniel is in the KMOX studio in St. Louis).

BRENNAN: I suppose it's your love of theaters as well as your desire to renovate downtowns that I guess you decided to become a man who pushes
the restoration of theaters around the country, Paul Westlake?

WESTLAKE: Downtowns *work* because of *concentrations* of people. So the thing
that's wonderful about theater is that it brings people onto the streets.
They use the city. Incredible *spin-offs* result from that. So, the reason we
are passionate about them (theaters) is that they are the catalysts that
make our urban neighborhoods work.

DANIEL: Now, you walked through Kiel Opera House. The major question is:

BRENNAN: His partner, Peter van Dijk did.

DANIEL: From your understanding of his view, what's the sense whether or
not it can be renovated?

WESTLAKE: Well the building is in great shape, comparatively. We've worked on over 30 older, pre-Depression palaces and arts facilities around the country. This one is in really good shape. From a physical standpoint and it is certainly do-able. And, we would think that St. Louis with that metropolitan population certainly deserves more arts facilities.

Other major cities from Seattle to Cleveland, and we can give you a list of ten of them, have multiple venues for the arts and you certainly could support it when you were a smaller population in the 20's and 30's. The arts have continuously grown across the United States. You (St. Louis) have grown in metropolitan population. The market should be there to do it.

BRENNAN: You look at other cities as small as Louisville with theater downtown and as big as New York City with Broadway. Both have counted on their economic success thanks to theater in their downtowns.

WESTLAKE: Right, many cities have seen that as a critical difference. You know Playhouse Square?

BRENNAN: Cleveland?

WESTLAKE: Right, Cleveland really turned that city around. But, Cleveland of course relies on a collection of cultural facilities. It's that tapestry of the arts that makes it work. It's not just Playhouse Square, wonderful Cleveland Playhouse and University Circle and just a constellation of alternative performing arts and fine arts venues, downtown. And, they re-enforce each other. They are very complementary.

Arts beget the Arts. And that has been largely been responsible for corporate recruitment and retention and for the economics downtown, and certainly the revitalization of Cleveland downtown is catalyzed to the spark that Playhouse Square gave through the renovation of its theaters in the '70s and '80s.

DANIEL: And yet Paul, in St. Louis, the issue of market saturation, theater saturation, has certainly come up as to whether or not with the Fox and Grandel Square and the like, would the Kiel Opera House survive?

WESTLAKE: We don't find in our metropolitan areas arts really competing with arts.

We find arts complementing arts. And, Kiel Opera House is a venue that allows different things to happen than the Fox. And I think this is the thing I think you have to understand.

DANIEL: Explain that, more.

WESTLAKE: Well, Kiel Opera House. First of all that building has the opportunity to be a performing arts center. Events centers, unlike most arts facilities in the United States. It had originally seven major areas for activities. You have the 3500 seat Opera House, one of the great music halls in America. It had four small theaters, flat floored, which gave them great flexibility to accommodate dance events, recitals, parties, dinner theater, exhibitions. Each is about 55 by 85 feet with ceilings about 30 feet high – each with its own separate access.

It has its grand lobby. It also had an exposition hall at the lower level which could host major museums and art shows and events like that, things like festivals and multiple activities can occur at Kiel. In fact, a lot of uses that are not traditional performing arts uses, and the kinds of things that happen in the Opera House itself can be very different from the Fox.

BRENNAN: So, you would not be concerned that St. Louis already has the 10,000 seat summer theater called the Muny. It has the Fox for winter and summer. It has a Stages musical theater in Kirkwood, not to mention the Repertory theater in Webster Groves—that re-opening Kiel Opera House we wouldn't be doing too much with too few people?

The Kiel could be a wonderful place for natural sound, for not having to rely on amplified sound as you have to in major Broadway shows. It is one of the few theaters in the country where you can have a full orchestra and not require it to be miked, so you can have good acoustics for the hall.

You can do grand opera, you can do certain types of Broadway things and revivals that don't require amplified sound. You have one of the most incredible stages in America. And then you have to think that it's more than the main hall. You have to think of all the event spaces that surround it that could allow for a constellation of activities—an environment that is very, very different from the other venues in St. Louis that are complementary.

DANIEL: Let's talk about the bottom line and that's money. How have other cities funded their renovation of theaters.

WESTLAKE: Normally these are cast at the outset as private and public partnerships. Take Cleveland as an example. Cuyahoga County had a tremendous investment in these theaters. And, we find in our work across the country that it is normally a partnership of the public sector, community leaders and the private sector and foundations.

We have, maybe out of 30 facilities we've worked on, perhaps two which have been completely privately funded. Normally the reason that the public sector is jumping into the fray is that they understand the economic advantages and revitalization potential that comes from these downtown venues: the *multiplier* effect.

The venues themselves may have kind of a thin bottom line, barely make a profit, lose a little bit of money. But the spin-offs are tremendous. The impact of Playhouse Square, which has $77 million in ticket revenue, may have $300 million in economic impact a year in Cleveland.

BRENNAN: We have to say good bye. But thank you very much for your thoughts on Kiel Opera House and here in St. Louis, from northeastern Ohio, Paul Westlake, Jr. Commissioner of Architecture, United States Institute of Theater Technology. Thanks for joining us on KMOX.

WESTLAKE: Thank you.

Bookend End 2007

In ever widening concentric circles from St. Louis in all directions—cities and towns from coast-to-coast and Gulf to Great Lakes offer downtown performing arts centers. St. Louis does not. Kiel Opera House is still stonewalled. The Muny is choked down to 50 nights a summer. St. Louis loses $350 million a year in *entertainment-driven* revenue. Westlake gave us the 'straight dope' ten years ago.

Kiel Opera House is still closed.

Chapter Fifteen

❦━✦━❦

Tourism and Other Cities

Since Kiel Opera House was closed in 1991, 200 cities and towns have built and opened new downtown performing arts centers or restored and reopened old ones. Killing Kiel costs the St. Louis region at least $300 million a year in entertainment-driven revenue. Here is where the business is going and why:

Baltimore's **Hippodrome**. Opened in 1914 and was closed in 1990. In 2004 it re-opened as the France-Merrick Performing Arts Center—three historic buildings and a new one.

Boston's **Opera House**. A downtown theater opened in 1928 underwent $38 million restoration and re-opened in July of 2004 *re-making* Boston's lower Washington Avenue. The National Trust extended *Most Endangered Eleven* status to the theater.

Buena Park, California. **Cerritos Center** opened in 1993. The 17,000 sq. ft. auditorium transforms into a 13,000 seat lyric for opera, an arena for touring shows and dance. A 1,600-seat concert hall with proscenium stage is set up for pop artists and classical performers. A 940-seat drama for plays, and a 1,700 seat theater-in-the-round.

Chicago's **Opera House** underwent a $100 million upgrade in 1992–1993. Three-weeks Wagner festivals, a decade apart, grossed $10 million on property and filled downtown hotels, motels and restaurants with show/hotel packages.

Cincinnati's **Arnoff Center**, downtown, contains three theater/concert halls, rehearsal areas and event space. Music Hall, downtown, is the home of Cincinnati Opera.

Cleveland's **Playhouse Square**. Four theaters served by central ticketing. The fourth—The Allen—reopened in 1997. Downtown Cleveland is a preferred tourist destination. Credit visionary Ray Shepardson, Junior League and Cleveland Foundation.

Denver Center for Performing Arts is credited as THE catalyst for downtown Denver's revitalization. Denver and Cayouga County receive 2.2 million a year on ticket tax alone. DCPA was the catalyst for Denver's building a new and larger convention center.

Des Moines' new **Civic Center** (Main Hall and Stoner Studio Theater) downtown, draws 250,000 a year, mostly in the wintertime, and creates hotel and motel business for Greater Des Moines.

Detroit's **Opera House** opened in 1922 as the Capitol Theater. A $21 million renovation prepared her for reopening in 1993. Home of Michigan Lyric Opera.

Ft. Lauderdale's new **Broward Performing Arts Center** (2700-seat Au-Rene Theater and 590-seat Amaturo) is the jewel of downtown. $52 million. Broward and The Parker Playhouse, also downtown, present musicals, blues, jazz, opera, ballet and plays.

Ft. Wayne's Performing Arts Center and historic **Embassy Theater** operate downtown, drawing year 'round.

Houston offers a 17-block downtown theater district. **The Alley Theater, Hobby Center**, Jones Hall for the Performing Arts, Verizon Wireless Theater, and the Wortham help fill downtown hotel and motel rooms, restaurants and retail outlets.

Kansas City has restored its historic Music Hall downtown and will open the stunning **Kauffman Center for Performing Arts** in 2010. League of Historic America Theaters 2005 tour celebrated seven Kansas City area historic theaters, built in the early 1900s, and operational today. The downtown Lyric is home of Kansas City Opera.

Los Angeles' **Disney Concert Hall**. October 20, 2003 LA opened the 2,265-seat Walt Disney, the fourth venue of The Music Center. $274 million. The Disney includes a 3,000 sq. ft. museum. It is the new home of the LA Philharmonic and Los Angeles Master C. on.

Madison Wisconsin. **Overture Center for the Arts,** ($300 million) is home to Madison Symphony, Opera, Ballet, Wisconsin Chamber Orchestra, Kanopy Dance, Madison Rep. Madison Family Theater, Wisconsin Academy of Sciences, Arts and Letters. (Downtown).

Memphis, Tennessee. **Cannon Center for Performing Arts** and the **Orpheum Theater** help draw conventions, travel groups and locals to downtown Memphis, year 'round.

Milwaukee's **Center for Performing Arts,** downtown, is home of Milwaukee Symphony, Florentine Opera, City Ballet Theater, Milwaukee Ballet.

Minneapolis. The new **Guthrie on the River** opened in July, 2006. The Twin Cities capture more convention, group travel and travel-for-entertainment business.

Nashville's **Tennessee Performing Arts Center** offers three theaters and Tennessee State Museum. Ballet, opera, and repertory company are resident-users. T-PAC brings in shows and concerts, and hosts special events. It cross-promotes with Opryland and the Nashville Convention Center. In 2006, Nashville opened a new Symphony Hall, downtown.

Newark's **New Jersey Performing Arts Center** is called the most significant economic *engine* in revitalizing downtown Newark. She opened in 1996, offering two theaters, a cabaret space, and support facilities.

Omaha's **Orpheum**, built in 1927, was renovated for $10 million in 2002 and quickly overbooked. This led to Omaha building The Holland Performing Arts Center, which opened in the Fall of 2005.

Orlando is building **Orlando Performing Arts Center,** contracting with Hines of Houston. Hines developed The Wortham Theater in Houston and Walt Disney Concert Hall in Los Angeles.

Paducah, Kentucky. **Luther F. Carson Four Rivers Center.** Downtown. Opened February 2004—A collaboration of private industry, foundations and 14 counties. 98,000 sq.ft. Philadelphia. **Kimmel Center**– $250 million dollar complex (Verizon Hall, Perelman Theater, Innovation Studio and Merck Arts Education Center). The Kimmel is home for eight resident companies including Philadelphia Orchestra, Opera and Ballet. Downtown.

Pittsburgh. Downtown Cultural District offers the Benedum Center for Performing Arts, Byham Theater, Heinz Hall (home of Pittsburgh Symphony) The O'Reilly Theater, and Harris Theater. Live arts give Pittsburgh a big downtown in the wintertime.

Salina Kansas' **Stiefel Theater for the Performing Arts** brings people to Salina during the wintertime to create business for hotels, motels, restaurants and retail outlets. She is an exciting gathering place for the region and delivers tax revenue to the City and State.

Salt Lake City. **The Rose Wagner Center** (Black Box—opened in 1979), Jeanne Wagner Theater (2001), Studio Theater (2002) is a great example of public/private partnership. Also operating in downtown Salt Lake are **Abravanel Hall** (home of the Salt Lake Symphony) and **The Capitol Theater** (built in 1913, restored and reopened in October 1978.)

San Francisco's **Opera House** (War Memorial), quake-damaged in 1992 was repaired, retrofitted for earthquake, and re-opened in 18 months. $88 million.

San Jose, California re-opened The **California Theater** in Sept. 2005 following a $73 million restoration. The theater had been closed for 31 years.

Santa Fe's **Opera Co.** is world-renowned. Santa Fe operates two other theaters with back-to-back stages. Santa Fe *presents* an 80-block cultural/ entertainment district.

Seattle's **Benaroya Hall**, a 2500-seat theater/concert hall and a 514-seat recital hall was built for $121 million. Benaroya family initially contributed 15.7. Benaroya opened in 1997. Seattle has since renovated its Opera House.

Topeka, Kansas **Performing Arts Center**, opened in 1991—a 2,500-seat theater/concert hall, black box theater, and festival hall for banquets and receptions. $6.2 million This was renovation of the old Municipal Auditorium. Ben Vereen and Judy Kay in *"On Broadway"* drew two sold-out crowds to open the theater.

Tucson boasts a **70-block** cultural district. Tulsa's **Performing Arts Center**—five theaters and a large reception hall—draws a million people a year.

Washington DC's **Kennedy Center** hosts 3,300 performances, events, festivals annually. Opera House renovated in 2004. DC offers several other theaters and concert halls. ue.

Wichita KS. **Orpheum Theater**, 2200 N. Broadway, opened in 1922 is undergoing major restoration by Orpheum Performing Arts Centre Ltd. The Orpheum was placed on The National Register in 1980. **Century Two Concert Hall at** 225 West Douglas is home of Music Theater of Wichita. Also downtown: Cabaret Old Towne, Mosley Street Melodrama, Stage One, Wichita's Children's Theater and Dance Center.

Kiel Opera House is still closed.

Chapter Sixteen

'Hall For Sale' Follow The Money

Pressures on public officials to facilitate crooked deals are applied, administration to administration to administration. Money or the threat of withholding money is one of their weapons.

"If you press us (Civic Progress) on the Opera House they might withhold support from future projects."

Walter Metcalfe, Bryan Cave

Part of every dollar given to City officials and candidates is to keep Kiel closed to protect the Fox. I assign a fairly high percentage to this. You can assign your own percentage. My analysis comes from a three-month study of Missouri Ethics Commission reports covering a small number of politicians over a limited period if time.

The payoffs to candidates, officials and campaigns are in addition to the money spent on the studies. Civic Progress companies, subsidiaries and divisions, Family members, law firms, accounting firms, contractors, and suppliers often give to the maximum allowed by law. A lot of this money controls where we can or cannot Go to enjoy music, arts and culture.

Is this discovery or reasonable cause for investigations? That's the idea.

Stonewall re-opening of Kiel Opera House, gut it for re-use

Francis Slay–Pres. Board of A., Candidate Mayor, Mayor	98,915
Darlene Green, Comptroller Incumbent	35,477
Freeman Bosley, Jr. Former Mayor, Mayoral Candidate	61,302

Clarence Harmon, Candidate for Mayor and Mayor   97,443

Alderman Mike McMillian Nineteenth ward Grand Center 36,540
    Total   *230,762*

Records of political contributions show dramatic upsurges when there is renewed interest in the Opera House such as formation and efforts of Kiel For Performing Arts, submission of business plans, petition drives. The money stonewalls it all. Upsurges in contributions occurred around the time of the *studies*. Jack Danforth heavily funded the studies through his foundation, and St. Louis 2004. Upsurges in contributions occur during campaigns. All candidates and major office holders are *taken care of equally* to *waste* The Opera house to protect Grand Center.

Patterns reveal the collaborators who have decided Kiel will *go down*. In using money to influence politicians, The Kiel deal became a *model* for the ballpark deal.

FRANCIS SLAY, ALDERMANIC PRESIDENT, MAYOR

1. Stolar Partnership–Harvey Harris, Fox Theater   8,250
2. Fox Theater Officers and Employees   1,425
3. Grand Center, Union Station, Kerth, SLU, Staff   3,940
4. Husch-Eppenberger   9,450
5. Bryan Cave, Walter Metcalfe, Kiel Partner's Attorney 8,250
6. Lashy-Baer John Arnold, Downtown Now   5,000
7. McCormack Baron Museum Plan   1,375
8. Kiel Partners Mark Sauer, CEO   1,000
9. Civic Progress/Kiel Partners Companies (26/19)   66,675
    Total   *98,915*
10. Thompson Coburn Armstrong Teasdale, others

DARLENE GREEN, COMPTROLLER

11. Stolar Partnership–(Harvey Harris–Fox Theater   2,850
12. Fox Theater Officers and Employees

13. Grand Center–Union Station, Kerth, SLU Staff,   2,300

14. Husch-Eppenberger   6,800

15. Bryan Cave. Walter Metcalfe, Kiel Partners Attorney   1,175

16. Lashy-Baer (John Arnold, Downtown Now)   2,000

17. McCormack Baron   4,500

18. Kiel Partners Mark Sauer, CEO   2,500

19. Civic Progress/Kiel Partners Companies (26/19)   17,252

   Total   *35,477*

20. Thompson Coburn, Armstrong Teasdale, others

Darlene Green was persuaded to have a study done to get rid of the Opera House. The 41 members of the study committee were dominated by Kiel Partners, Grand Center, Civic Progress. It was a biased study. Consultants were pre-instructed to come in and report what the study sponsor wanted: to gut the Opera House.

FREEMAN BOSLEY, JR. MAYOR AND CANDIDATE

1. Stolar Partnership   400

2. Fox Theater   1,177

3. Husch Eppenberger   5,125

4. Grand Center   3,250

5. Bryan Cave   1,375

6. Lashly Baer   7,750

7. McCormack Baron   3,600

8. Civic Progress/Kiel Partners   38,625

   Total   *61,302*

9. Thompson Mitchell then Coburn, Armstrong Teasdale, others.

CLARENCE HARMON CANDIDATE/MAYOR/CANDIDATE

1. Stolar Partnership	4,490
2. Fox Theater	2,750
3. Husch Eppenberger	450
4. Fleishman Hillard – 1997 studies 'look the other way'	5,900
5. Grand Center	4,175
6. Bryan Cave	3,100
7. Lashly Baer Arnold fund raiser at Fox	10,532
8. McCormack Baron	8,100
9. Kiel Center/Blues	2,000
10. Civic Progress/Kiel Partners	59,987
Total	*97,443*

11. Thompson Mitchell, Armstrong Teasdale, Foundations others.

1997–98 was the *time* to get rid of Kiel—three expensive studies—ULI, 2004, Smithsonian—all with the same purpose. Fleishmann-Hillard coordinated. Grand Center was involved in all three. Danforth put in big dollars. City officials were paid to participate and/or to look the other way. The goal was to move Kiel onto the Downtown Now Plan for gutting and re-use. When the *powers* decide on an initiative, they blitz it with money, when they want to kill an initiative, they kill it with money. Officials and candidates are paid off equally.

Alderman Mike McMillan, Nineteenth Ward, took in big money from the *gut the Opera House* crowd, ULI task force members, Civic Progress/Kiel Partners, the Fox, Grand Center SLU, law firms

1. Grand Center/Fox Theater, Fox Associates	5,676
2. St. Louis University: Officers, Board, Employees	3,575
3. Civic Progress/Kiel Partners	10,240
4. Law Firms Representing the Above	8,575
5. Misc. Consultants, Operatives, other politicians	8,425
Total	*36,540*

These are unprecedented levels of contributions to a city alderman. They *clustered* around the time of the Kill Kiel studies. Contributors are the same: Civic Progress, Kiel Partners, their banks and law firms, Grand Center, the Fox, St. Louis University. The studies and payoffs were to signal the end of Kiel Opera. The RCGA, The Danforth Foundation, Nations/Boatman's and Kiel Partners would pay for its gutting. A few St. Louisans stood up and said NO. Payoffs continue. Vince Schoemehl is at the helm of Grand Center. Attacks on Kiel are unlikely to stop.

Political scientists and news reporters try to analyze City politics. Follow the money.

Bookend End 2007

Going back to Schoemehl's administration, at least $5 million has been given to politicians to do away with Kiel Opera House. That is why mayors from Schoemehl to Bosley to Harmon to Slay have either closed it or stonewalled its reopening.

Kiel Opera House is still closed.

CHAPTER SEVENTEEN

TO PRESERVE — ATTACK

Kiel Opera House does not need preserving. It is not canned fruit. Upgrade and reopen it. *Preservationists must do more than preserve.* Preservations *climb mountains* to save or bring back historic resources. There were mountains behind mountains to climb to save Kiel Opera House. The moment Kiel Partners announced it would not restore and re-open Kiel, it should have been placed on The *National Register*. No one bothered to do that for four years.

In 1999, Kiel For Performing Arts kicked in $1,000 *to get Landmarks going.* Lynne Josse created a spectacular submission. Carolyn Toft walked it through the St. Louis approval process. Claire Blackwell moved it from the state to federal. Kiel Opera House was placed on the National Register of Historic Places in February of 2000. Listing on the Register doesn't save a building. It helps. Coral Courts Motel on Route 66 was on The Register but it was torn down in the mid '90s. Our understanding of the National Register designation is that it:

a.) prevents federal funds from being used to destroy a building

b.) makes available historic tax credits for restoration

c.) brings favorable publicity to a threatened building

Were we wrong?

THE TRUE PLIGHT OF THE PRESERVATIONIST

It is the last of the ninth, two out. You are at the *plate* with a count of two strikes and no balls. Randy Johnson peers in. He's is in the sun, you're in the shade.

Why do we (preservationists) start out at such a disadvantage?

1. The deals/agreements/contracts to destroy or *re-use* an historic building are done behind closed doors, often with concurrence of officials who are sworn to protect these buildings, often with the knowledge of the media.

2. Deals are *spun*, under-communicated, and sometimes never communicated.

3. Money has been spread around to *insure* the deal. Millions were spent in misinformation campaigns and biased studies to convince the St. Louis region it did not need Kiel Opera House, or that it could be turned into a museum or museums.

4. The people are *conditioned* by publicity lauding the benefits of the proposed destruction, modification, re-use.
    We are going to bring a Smithsonian. Cardinals World will save downtown. Or, the people are threatened: *We'll move out . There will be no Kiel deal unless we get a garage.*

5. We are *reacting.* The opposition has been on the attack for some time.

6. Architects make more money re-designing for re-use. So they remain silent. Financial institutions put more money *in play* with re-use than with restoration. Wrecking companies make more money destroying buildings and salvage. Construction companies and unions make more money on buildings than on restoring.

7. And we *waste* time and effort calling on the enemy. They are *all* the enemy.

To Preserve – Attack

1. Believe nothing anyone *says*. Do not believe there is a developer waiting in the wings to come forward as soon as the building is torn down. Get things in writing. Clip and organize articles in the newspapers. Same with radio and TV transcripts.

2. Believe little you read in the newspapers, they seldom get it right. Every day is a new day. The media has no sense of history or the future, they function in *today*. If you can find an aggressive reporter who wants to go after a Pulitzer Prize or a courageous lawyer, cut to the chase and go for it. No reporter has time to understand your cause.

3. Quickly develop a Preservation-*PLUS* message. Not just: *save an historic building*. Historic is passive. Save is passive. What are the *economic* benefits of saving/re-opening it? What are the *cultural* benefits? What are the *social* benefits? What are the *political* benefits? What are the *tourism* benefits?
   Preservationists must be *marketers*. (We constantly communicated the good-business of a re-opened Kiel Opera House, that it was not just an historic building but creates jobs, income, tax revenue and tourism.

4. *Communicate benefits* for all constituents involved with the *issue*. Vigorously communicate benefits to each constituent and to the public. What are concrete benefits in saving/renovating the building. How will it contribute?

Sell Features and Benefits

The Opera House will add at least *one-fourth gross revenue* to Kiel Center and increase the City's tax revenue (tickets, food, beverage, earnings etc.)

The Opera House would give theater groups *places* to perform.

The Opera House complex will provide *internships* for college students in many disciplines—same building.

The Kiel Opera House gives tourism promoters a year 'round blockbuster. Keeping the promise restores *credibility* to other projects. Credibility leads to support. You will receive a *return* on your investment. Union Station needs the help Kiel can provide.

If they still ignore the win, win, win, messages – *sue the bastards*.

5. Blend into your features/benefits – successes or similar projects from other cities. You may not be believed. But, let them hear it from *someone else*.

6. *Never* ever give up. Don't listen to 'you can't win'.

Those who discount you are usually afraid you will win. Take a break, re-group, but never give up. Watch your back.

7. Don't leave it up to officials or agencies, or people with power. *You* can effect change as an individual or a group.

December 24, 1999
Seeks *Endangered Status for Kiel Opera House*

Stating that Kiel Opera House remains in great danger, Edward L. Golterman today applied for inclusion of the Opera House in National Trust's 2000 list of Eleven Most-Endangered Historic Places.

"I believe the Opera House meets all criteria for being an historic treasure and for being endangered. It was the victim of damage and looting early on; of phony, biased studies aimed at destroying or crippling its use as a large music venue (museum plans); and will be controlled by another sports entity. "To me those are dangers," said the grandson of one of Kiel's founders, Guy Golterman.

"The efforts of the Fox Theater to eliminate this possible source of competition are on-going. The biggest threat is the lack of will or courage on the part of City officials to not only rescue this treasure but apply it vigorously to downtown revitalization, as other cities do."

Golterman says he believes the National Trust for Historic Preservation can bring strong resources not only to preserve it but to reopen it. Re-opening Kiel Opera House is clearly the will of the people, because they know what it can do for our downtown economy. It is not the will of the monopolists. Submissions from private citizens are welcomed.

8. Meet all outside consultants as they come off the airplane and put them right back on their plane. Outside consultants know what they are going to recommend *before* they come in. It has to do with who is *paying* them. Be wary of *feasibility* studies. These are undertaken to wait you out. They are delay tactics.

Calling on the Enemy is a waste of time. They are *all* the enemy.

For Immediate Release June 19, 2000
Kiel Opera House – '*Eleven Most Endangered*'
Resubmit For 2001

The Kiel Opera House missed this year's list of America's Eleven Most-Endangered Historic Places, but St. Louisan Ed Golterman will re-nominate the Opera House for the 2001 listing by the National Trust for Historic Preservation.

"In the '90s, we lost The Kiel Convention Hall, The Arena, The Ambassador Building and Ambassador Theater. *The Opera House was damaged, remains closed and under attack. Of course, I'm going to re-submit,*" he added.

From the National Trust's David Brown in Washington D.C.: *Opera House would not be among the eleven announced on June 26th.*

Bookend End 2007

Preservationists are in *wars*, make no mistake about it. There are mountains behind mountains, walls behind walls, and nothing is at it appears. We can't play *nice*. Trust no one. What has and has not happened to Kiel Opera House is an extensive study of *multiple threats* and clandestine strategies.

December 13, 2000, author re-submits Opera House for consideration toward listing on Eleven Most Endangered historic places for 2001. Author again asks the National Trust to engage the battle. The Kiel Opera House was not included in the list of most endangered, but the National Trust included a *generic*' category for old theaters. Author did not re-submit for 2002.

In St. Louis, preservationists lack the courage to go to war. Landmarks had to be prodded to seek National Historic Place status for the Opera House. That's fear, kids.

At year's end, The Old Post Office has been given official *blessing* as the historic building downtown. The Old Post Office can not bring 800,000 people a year downtown nor deliver $6 million a year in tax revenue as can Kiel Opera House. But, the Old Post Office does not "threaten" the Fox Theater. So, it is a "safe" restoration project.

The author and his group did not help get it on the Register to give the Fox Theater, Mark Sauer and the Lauries historic tax credits to gut it, or, for the Fox to get a piece of it. Re-opening Kiel Opera House would be an *honorable, and economically beneficial use of historic tax credits.*

The National Trust extended to an old downtown Boston theater—'Most endangered' status in 1995. The Boston Opera House today is a glittering addition to downtown Boston and an economic engine. Clear Channel, or whatever it is called now, is hauling a lot of money out of Boston Opera House.

Kiel Opera House is still closed.

Chapter Eighteen

Selective Misunderstanding

S elective misunderstanding is a *tool* of the closed-minded, the fearful, the disinterested. *If we pretend to misunderstand we don't have to help.*

"Oh... you want to save the Kiel Opera House" No

"Save" implies it just sits there and people look at it. We want to restore and re-open it, create *jobs, income, benefits, revenue and bring lots of people* downtown. It took a year to dispel this misunderstanding.

"Oh... you want to spend a lot of tax money???"

No, we would use private funding and create jobs, income, benefits, and tax revenue for the City. In a public/private partnership the City may want to have a stake in the great financial benefits. The financial mechanism for a restored Kiel Opera House always has been *private* investors, naming/sponsorship/licensing and some historic tax credits. May be a little tourism money. *No* long-term public debt.

Multiple use of the Opera House and turnover of some of the venues more than once in a day will add one-fourth to the *gross* revenue of the block known as Kiel Center, at least $40 million dollars a year. That is *taxable* revenue to help city services. Cultural, theater-going tourists bring a good deal of money into downtown economies.

"Oh... you want to return it to its former glory."

No, we want to prepare and market all the spaces that never were totally used. We are looking to the future, to get the maximum cultural, entertainment and economic return from this building. The city never knew what it had, doesn't know now.

"Oh... you want do Opera there??"

We want to provide opportunities for *all* performance groups, for all types of music, dance, civic and cultural festivals and displays and educational activity. It is a civic building for all of the people. Open booking.

"It will hurt the Fox."

No, it will grow the market, drawing more people to downtown St. Louis by offering choices. We are more attractive to booking organizations. Only the Fox says it will hurt the Fox.

"It will hurt Kiel Center."

No, the Opera House awakens the great Market Street expanse. It does different things than Kiel Center. This is *Plus* business.

"Oh... you live in the past, you're dreamers."

No, we have a business/marketing plan that will help downtown's future. We have a professional team to do this.

"You don't have any money."

We don't need all the money. We have the financing plan that provides a return on investment and spreads costs among several parties that can benefit from the project.

"You're going to hurt the new performing arts center at UMSL."

No, we are going to help revitalize downtown St. Louis. A revitalized downtown helps the entire region. A depressed downtown hurts the region. We can *outreach* to UMSL.

"It's too big for our group to use."

There are six venues within The Building, they are not all the same size.

"People are afraid to come downtown."

Are people less afraid to go to Grand Center? Millions of people come downtown for sporting events. A brightened and energized Market Street would draw.

"The powers that be don't want it."

Perhaps. That simply means that new leadership is needed. I experienced this from the media, from so-called leaders and from ordinary citizens. The powers-that-be haven't brought back downtown. In St. Louis, proponents of plans and ideas that are not 'blessed' by Civic Progress are discounted and ridiculed, particularly in the media.

They are selective and deliberately misunderstood. For more than five years, I (we) tried every day to tell the *good business* story of a re-opened Kiel Opera House in a struggling downtown.

"Oh, you want to save the Kiel Opera House".

Look at our plan. Look at our Mission Statement. It's all There. If your message is misunderstood it's usually because the 'receiver' wants to misunderstand it.

September 1998 Mission Statement

To Bring World Class entertainment to St. Louis while nurturing and *incubating* St. Louis-based talent and performing groups.

To create jobs, income, wages and revenues during renovation and 'quantum leap' these economic benefits in operation of the complex.

To welcome all to this civic institution, as a place of-the-people.

To propel downtown St. Louis and the region as a preferred cultural tourist destination.

To inspire through music. To energize through dance.

To challenge through drama. To relax through comedy.

To enrich and educate through exhibits and outreach.

To care for this St. Louis treasure forever...

February 16, 2000
Riverfront Times
Operatic Tenor

Regarding the February 9 *State of the Arts* column on the dearth of performing arts space: Let's forget the word 'Opera" for a moment. OK?

There is a 500,000 sq. ft magnificent building in our core downtown that includes one of the world's finest main theaters and at least four (two stacked theater/auditoriums) on either side for up to five simultaneous performance capabilities; plus special events, party, exhibit and civic-event spaces down below. Where is the *space* problem?

Kind of like a Kennedy Center, only better. Kind of like Tennessee Performing Arts Center in Nashville, only better. Like Cleveland's Playhouse Square, in one building.

It can *house* many performing arts groups, theater groups, dance groups and help them market, produce and draw. It can bring 1.2 million people a year into a pitiful-ass downtown that offers nothing. It can return to St. Louis, from a 300-mile radius–the two-night stay, year 'round theater-going tourist who now goes to Chicago, Louisville, Nashville, Tulsa, Milwaukee, Cleveland, Memphis, etc. And, how many years in a row will the country's silver hairs want to go back to Branson?

It does not need a philanthropist, but a group of business people who actually want a return on their investment. The 57 naming opportunities in the building will give St. Louis its first truly healthy private endowment for the arts.

The 2004 and ULI studies were commissioned, controlled and paid for by the Fox, Grand Center, and Kiel Partners with the sole purpose of destroying the Opera House' main theater.

We are the only city in the country without a performing arts center in its core downtown. This is an extensive study of multiple threats and clandestine strategies. Think Big. St. Louis cannot afford to think small any longer.

The P-D has gone silent on the Opera House. The Cardinals are touting their new stadium, something called Chouteau's Pond is proposed for just south of the existing stadium. The Opera House remains threatened. The enemy is time, and the silence of the Lauries. Both are news.

February 1, 2000

Mr. Dick Thomas–President
Paige Sports Entertainment
7700 Bonhomme Avenue
Clayton, MO 63105

Win, Win, Win
    Ok...let's make this win-win for everyone:
    For Mark Sauer: a pedestrian walkthrough of, but not through the music hall.
    For Darlene Green a Blues-Jazz experience on the 15th Street side. I've had an architect render a very exciting "Blues-Jazz" experience.
    Larry Williams (treasurer) gets another garage.
    The Mayor gets re-elected: Super Bowl and the Opera House. Not bad for civic pride.
    The Lauries get revenue: van Dijk Pace and Westlake would manage restoration.

Regards,
cc Don Landers

Dick Thomas is the Laurie's attorney and President of Paige Sports Entertainment. Don Landers is their Accountant in Columbia, Missouri.
    Thomas to author: *"I don't have time to consider your letters, but would find them amusing."*

Are we (you) misunderstood? Of course. Is it intentional? Of course. Why? Fear or laziness, or both. If you understand the message you have to confront the fear. That is uncomfortable. If you overcome the fear, then you have to act, and there is real or perceived danger in acting. It is much easier to misunderstand, and much safer.

Does selective misunderstanding help the City of St. Louis? No

After two years of presenting proposals and business plans that did not call on the Lauries to invest a huge amount in the Opera House, Thomas, wrote: *"The Lauries have no intention of making a huge investment in the Kiel Opera."*

October 2001 *Riverfront Times* awarded author best one-man band of the year. The story keeps the issue before the people but labels the author "pretty much a *gadfly* and a pain in the ass." The last line read: but he's right. When the author described the Harris McCoole plan to gut the Opera House as *criminal* he was described in the P-D as a *preservationist. Selective Misunderstanding.*

The Century Building was destroyed in 2004, Busch Stadium in 2005. *Kiel Opera House is still closed.*

Chapter Nineteen

Progress?? It's Still There Hanging On

The Kill-the-Kiel studies of 1998–2000 didn't do it. Three dots on the Opera House outline were just dots on a transparency. The Kiel Opera House was not gutted during the late 1990s, as Civic Progress directed. It has survived through 2007.

Supporters for re-opening the opera house achieved much when we stayed *on task*. Fear stalled progress. Kiel For Performing Arts, incorporated in September 1998. We were to build a team in all disciplines required—restoration, marketing, finance, theater operation. We would rattle cages, for a while, then hopefully convince all that this is simply *good business*. We had the plan and the people to do this. We were never to be just a citizens group, or an awareness group.

Before Running Out of Gas

K-FPA battled the phony studies to a standstill, raised regional awareness of a regional resource and drew spport. But, without the lease we could not raise money.

"Don't even waste your time by applying."

Lynn Barth, Monsanto Fund

"We are funding only projects approved by the Downtown Now Plan."
Bruce Anderson, Danforth Foundation.

Anderson and his foundation could fund the destruction of the Opera House, but not its restoration and reopening.

This was the pattern of response from Foundations. They would not go against Civic Progress. They would protect the Fox. The litany of turn-downs is pretty boring.

The Regional Arts Commission did award us $5,000. $1,000 went to get Landmarks moving on National Register status. And, we paid a good attorney to prepare a lease.

Pure and Simply–A War

There have been on-going collaborations to destroy Kiel Opera House. K-FPA was just getting in the way, temporarily. By December 1999, when I saw no movement on the part of the new lease holders, Grand Center send Tom Reeves downtown to stonewall. I because frustrated and aggressive. The K-FPA board, or members of the board, became fearful, backed down from the mission, and we split.

"Ed pisses people off". Yes, that was part of the 'walk', part of the plan.

People and institutions that were never going to be challenged were challenged. They have not played nice. Nice does not do it.

KIEL AUDITORIUM IS GONE. WOLVES CIRCLE THE OPERA HOUSE

Russell Carter told me he cried the day they started tearing down Kiel Auditorium. I nearly cried the day they made a circus and media event out of imploding of the Arena. I'll be damned if the scumbags are going to destroy the Kiel Opera.

This is dishonorable business. You don't fight dishonorable business-nicely.

We were all warriors at the start and picked up warriors along the way, then warriors began dropping out or going in other directions. But before we split—progress:

- Collected 4,700+ signatures calling for re-opening the Kiel Opera House, presented these to city officials and to the new lease-holders for Kiel Center and the Opera House, Paige Sports Entertainment.

- Provided initial funding for Landmarks and historical background toward Kiel Opera House listed on the National Register of Historic Places.

- Author prepared and forwarded a submission to the National Trust For Historic Preservation to list the Kiel Opera House as one of "Eleven most endangered historic sites for 2,000." Opera House did not make list, nor was it selected in 2001.

- Gathered 300+ letters, faxes, and e-mails of support. Forwarded to leaseholder, City officials, and civic leaders.

- Obtained a support Resolution from the St. Louis Board of Aldermen.

- Took more than 100 people through the Opera House – potential investors, restorers, theatrical company operators, City officials, media, civic leaders.

- Communicated how other cities were using theaters—old and new to help spark downtown revitalization.

- Communicated the economic and cultural benefits and contribution to downtown revitalization—good business, not a charity.

- Submitted four business/marketing/financing plans to city and leaseholders.

- More than 200 speaking engagements, and special events before groups as well as media. Correspondence with office holders, arts and entertainment organizations, civic leaders, downtown business people, religious and cultural leaders and the media.

- Brought in Dinner Theater expert John Kinnamon and theater architect Peter van Dijk who toured the Opera House and came out with a "can do" message.

- Evan Schwartzfarb of Palm Capital Investments, Boca Raton developed a financing plan, bonds-bonds repaid out of operation of facility and naming/sponsorship.

- Countered the lies about the condition and capability of the Opera House and the positioning of St. Louis as a small town that could not support two large theaters.

- Got Kiel Opera House on the National Register of Historic Places.

KFPA Team: H. Russell Carter, Jeff and Elle Stewart, Bob Hutchings, Gary Bill, Joe Dubuque, Bill Neal, Peter Vaccaro, Monica McFee, Mike Tooley, Mike Henderson, Charlene Bry, Mallarie Zimmer. Later on Sam

Glaser, Chosan Nygen, Jim Heidenry, Elliot Liebson, Peggy Eggers, Diane Rosen, Gale Evans, Mary Lou Hudson. For the first two years of K-FPA, perhaps 25–30 served on the board. I apologize for those I missed.

Professional help was given by Ron O'Connor, Alan Steinberg, Tom Klein, Glen Jamboretz, John Kinnamon, Peter van Dijk, Paul Westlake, Jr. Willie Obermuehler, Evan Schwartzfarb and others. Performers and volunteers assisted at special events, fund raisers and petition gathering. That we were able to raise nearly $20,000 just to keep it going was an achievement in itself, on a project so opposed by the *powers*.

We opened the door for the powerful to walk through. We gave them all they needed to course-correct. If they had used all of the money they used (and continue to use to destroy the Opera House) to reopen it the Downtown Now plan would not be in such bad shape. But scumbags do not course-correct. They stay scumbags.

Stonewalled. During 2002 and 2003, the author asked St. Louis County to take leadership in seed-funding, obtaining lease and assigning author to build professional team to re-open Kiel Opera House by mid 2003, certainly in 2004.

BREAK WITH THE K-FPA BOARD, NOVEMBER 1999.

The Board was never important until we obtained funding and/or the project was adopted by the City. Until then we were kind of massaging each other from an organizational standpoint. That is not to say we were not working but the structure or organization was not the focus, at least for the author. I had seen enough of the system (15 years) and decided to continue on trying to effect real change. The Board feared my aggressiveness. Did I feel betrayed, let down? Yes. Is that important? No.

I resigned as chairman of Kiel For Performing Arts on November 28, 1999. People in St. Louis were tired of the 'behind closed doors' decisions and control over their lives. I believe they wanted change and everything put in the open. I had to continue to be a warrior.

K-FPA trusts Sauer. They staged a performing arts weekend downtown, and a fund raiser or two to raise *awareness*. The Lauries seem unmoved by any efforts, and not interested in the Opera House. Mark Sauer is still in control. Darlene Green is still in control. K-FPA has been conned and stonewalled.

Jim Heidenry, a true urban pioneer, and a tireless worker, died in September 2002.

Kiel For Performing Arts is a non-influence. They believed Clear Channel would restore and reopen the Opera House. They forgot the mission statement and wasted two years.

Bookend End 2007

We had opened the door for the powerful to walk back in and make it right. With the Opera House downtown St. Louis is a real downtown.

Scumbags do not course-correct. The author asked the St. Louis County Executive and County Council to take leadership, seed-fund and participate in bringing the Opera House back right, for the entire region. The push is for a new ballpark and casinos.

Kiel Historic Exhibit graced the lobby of the Adam's Mark during 2003 Fair St. Louis and the Millennium during Sister Cities International. But, visitors could not go into Kiel Opera House.

Kiel Opera House is still closed.

Chapter Twenty

Sue The xxxx

We heard this, a lot.

The 1992 lease described the Kiel Center Development project as creation of a civic center. Tax breaks and favorable bond rates were provided at least in part on the basis of historic restoration. Kiel Opera House restoration and re-opening was an integral part of the deal, and ballyhooed by Kiel Partners' to get the deal, and by Al Kerth as late as 1995 — *going to be done first class.*

A perfectly good 10,000-seat auditorium, with large meeting rooms and exhibit halls, was destroyed. *Nothing was restored.* The Kiel Opera House was cut off from the new building, damaged and looted and most of the loot taken out to warehouses in and around Grand Center for *storage* toward some future use. The Opera House stage was left open to the elements for 12–18 months depending on source. The load-in area was damaged. Thousands of cubic feet were taken from nearly every level: major space encroachment. This was major destruction of city property.

Kiel Center's load-in tunnel was *not* extended into the Opera House. INTENT. The parking garage provided no service to the Opera House. INTENT. Kiel Center opened in 1994, with the Opera House damaged, sealed off, and forgotten. A careful look at the original lease, the positioning of the new parking garage and not extending the Kiel Center load-in tunnel to the Opera House clearly indicate Kiel Partners were *never* going to re-open the Opera House. The physical evidence is and was undeniable — in any court action. There was no court action.

Nothing Good Cooks In a Cauldron of Fear

The City cringed. It feared loss of Civic Progress support on other projects. In 1995, an officer of The Land Clearance for Redevelopment Authority signed for the City that Kiel Partners had met its obligation by spending 2.5 million on repairs. As important as the sign-off are:

Well into 1995, legal action was not considered. The people and the City expected the restoring/re-opening of the Opera House. Then, abruptly Kiel Partners said no, they would not restore and re-open it. The Board of Aldermen had vigorous discussion, there was public outcry but, in the end, Kiel Partners *walked*. The actual announcement that Kiel Opera House would not be renovated was contained in an internal Kiel Center memo. The memo and the decision were kept from the public.

The memo made reference to the $19 million renovation of an old theater in downtown Detroit, and to the costs of building and operating Kiel Center. November 1994 work stopped. Alberici vacated the site. Several months later, BSI Constructors came in to *secure* the Opera House as best they could.

December 13, 1995. Citing the Master Lease Agreement of 1992, Associate City Counselor Fran Oates wrote Alderman Dan McGuire: Kiel Partners and the Land Clearance Authority have an obligation to restore Kiel Opera House. McGuire urged the City to sue Kiel Partners for reneging on their agreement. There were differing opinions within the City Counselor's Office and within other departments at City Hall. McGuire and others waged a year-long battle. The City declined to pursue in court, citing a 'certificate' of completion, relieving Kiel Partners of the responsibility, after they spent 2.5 million in damage repair. *We would be suing ourselves.* Cop-out.

August 1998, following the ULI exercise.

Citing the same certificate of completion, City Counselor Eric Banks recommends in August of 1998 that the City not sue Kiel Partners toward completion of the restoration. Banks acknowledged there were differences of opinion among attorneys in his office. The City Counselor decided they did not have a strong case and that it would be like suing *ourselves*. Others in his department felt they should pursue litigation. The City caved, let them off the hook.

Bryan Cave's Walter Metcalfe, Jr. a founder of Grand Center, and at least partial author of the "lease from hell" had this warning for the City:

'if you pursue the Kiel Opera House matter in court, you risk offending the "benevolent' support of Civic Progress on future projects'. In other words: 'we get our way and we'll keep the money spigot open'. Friendly warning, or extortion? The City backed down. One can only imagine the supportive role the Fox and Grand Center played in this dishonorable work.

Dan McGuire was named Parks Director, ending his pro-Kiel efforts.

August, 1998, City Counselor Eric Banks recommended against suing the operators of Kiel Center to get them to finish renovating the Opera House. Banks cited the December 1994 certificate of completion.

In 2000, the City refused to challenge the Lauries for a portion of the Kiel to SAVVIS naming-rights money. Mayor Harmon said *we might lose.*

Kiel Center has kept some air circulated, some electrical, and has done some repair work but time works against the *noble* building. The Opera House fell victim to the incompetence in operating the Kiel Center side.

Though there were complaints about the *rip-off* there was no legal action. The Kiel Opera House problem seemed of no concern to anyone until the author stood up at a Downtown Now Public meeting in February of 1998 and asked in a very loud voice.

Why is Kiel Opera House not on the Downtown Now Plan?

I am sure there were a few 'oh shits' among the officials and the consultants in the room. Or, 'is this guy nuts?'

At K-FPA events, meetings, fund-raisers, and in gathering petitions to re-open Kiel we heard it over and over: *Sue the Bastards.* The problem was (is) that the bastards should have been sued long ago. The criminal activity was neither exposed nor challenged by the media, the city, nor the civil and criminal justice agencies. Our objective in 1998 was to get the Opera House onto the Downtown Now Plan, get it renovated, and re-opened. We didn't have the money to sue.

The author saw a great civic, economic, and cultural resource being fed to the wolves and he began a multi-directional campaign to try to change that.

He wrote a letter calling for legal action and called on two law firms seeking a legal assessment and to see if any St. Louis law firm would go against Civic Progress. Anti-Trust, Destruction of Civic Property and Conflict-of-Interest seemed applicable. Both law firms claimed *conflict-of-interest.* But he also began building a team who also knew the value of a re-opened Kiel Opera House. They began telling the *value* story.

Calls for Investigations

Why must it be the City that sues, or citizens? Not our responsibility.

1. *August 17, 1998* – EG letter printed in St. Louis Business Journal calling for legal action and investigations, citing physical damage, anti-trust violations and conflicts of interest.

2. *September 21, 1998* – Correspondence and background information delivered to Tom Vandiver, Attorney with Sonnenchein, Nath and Rosenthal, 1 Metropolitan Square — 30 page business plan plus possible grounds for lawsuits: physical damage, anti-trust law violations, breaking of contracts, and conflicts of interest. Vandivers held the material for a few days but said they had a *conflict-of-interest*. I didn't know that Alan Bornstein, was working on gutting the Kiel Opera House for re-use by the Smithsonian.

3. *October 19, 1998* – Three-page request of *Post-Dispatch* publisher, Mike Pulitzer to assign an investigative reporter. No response.

4. *January 25, 1998* – Took basically the same document to an attorney in St. Louis County, looking for a lawyer not connected to Civic Progress, Kiel Partners, Grand Center. I was advised to proceed on a positive course, to convince decision-makers the Opera House was good business. Doors remained closed. And, the wolves were gathering.

5. *October 6, 1999* – Four-page letter to Attorney General Janet Reno to have newly appointed U.S. Attorney, Eastern and Southern Missouri investigate. In Appendix. No response.

6. *January 1, 2000* – Sent Janet Reno again, 11-page background and request to investigate. Text is in Appendix. No response.

7. *January 11, 2000* – Similar requests to Attorney General Reno, Melvin N. Price, Jr. Chief, Anti Trust Div. Justice Dept. Chicago; Jay Nixon, Missouri Attorney General; Circuit Attorney D. Joyce Hayes. No response. In Appendix.

8. *May 2, 2000* – Letter to Price, Audrey Fleissig, US. Attorney, Eastern Missouri. Copies to Missouri Attorney General Nixon. Another request to investigate, reference to previous correspondence. No response. In Appendix.

9. *January 2001* – Similar. No response.

10. *November 2002* – Similar. Citing the attacks on Kiel by the owners of the Fox, other Grand Center entities and their collaborators downtown.

Bookend End 2007

11. *September 2002* – citing the latest assault by the Fox Theater, the author again asked justice system jurisdictions to investigate.

12. *March 2003* – Author asks U.S. attorney to investigate the Fox Theater's role in the Breckenridge plan to reopen Kiel in 2005. No legal action planned or pending. Many of the 'players' are leaving— several have gone to Portland, Officials have left Grand Center and the symphony.

13. *2004–2005* – Author asked U.S. Attorney to file anti-trust litigation against all who have collaborated in the restraint-of-trade of Kiel Opera House. Ditto: 2006 and 2007.

Kiel Opera House is still closed.

CHAPTER TWENTY ONE

VINCE SCHOEMEHL AND SCHOEMEHL SPAWN

Three-term Mayor Vince Schoemehl (1980–1992) presided over a changing city and a deteriorating downtown. He raised money, passed out jobs and launched careers. Any politican who can win three terms is good. Was he a visionary? I don't know.

Was he a deal-maker? Yes. Schoemehl staffers, appointees, backers, advisors, since the early '80s are all over city, county and state government and agencies. Some of these agencies exist at least in part to promote business and tourism.

Sometime in the '80s, Vince, or someone representing him, assured the Fox Theater that Kiel Opera House was *nothing to worry about*. This is not just rumor. Four St. Louis City administrations have been well-rewarded for wasting Kiel Opera House.

In 2002, Schoemehl was named CEO of Grand Center. Why? Is he the arts czar recommended in the St. Louis 2004 cultural study?

SHORT LIST

- *J. Kim Tucci* – The Pasta House – early Schoemehl fund raiser/advisor. Kim has shifted attention to midtown Grand Center and St. Louis U. Board member, and a heavy Grand Center booster. As Chairman of St. Louis Convention and Tourism Commission, he loads up support for grand center, leaves Kiel Opera House dark and unused. County Council denied Tucci and Schoemehl tourism tax revenue to produce a promotional video for Grand Center.

- *Lou Hamilton* – Chairman of Missouri Tourism Commission. Hamilton keeps Opera House out of the tourism attraction mix. He wastes a six-event capable building in downtown St. Louis that could mean *work* for performers, musicians, special-events planners, caterers, etc. Lou is helping Vince keep his promise to Leon Strauss.

- *Kathleen Brady* – SLU Vice President, Facilities, and former Schoemehl staffer. Brady pulled University President Lawrence Biondi into the Urban Land Institute Task force.

- *Joanne LaSala* – former Schoemehl aide. Former President of St. Louis 2004 — the Danforth initiative. Joanne kept the Kiel Opera House out of the St. Louis 2004 plans.

- *Peter Sortino* – another Schoemehl-appointee, succeeded LaSala at 2004, and has done the same. He moved from 2004 to the Danforth Foundation.

- *Tom Irwin* – former head of Bi-State Transit, Tom is now Dick Fleming's sidekick at RCGA. Fleming has kept the Opera House out of the downtown revitalization plans. Irwin will *protect* Grand Center.

- *Dennis Coleman* – Director of Development, St. Louis County. Has never recognized the Opera House as a regional economic resource. The County throws money or extends tax breaks to ballparks, domes and casinos

Bookend End 2007

Schoemehl and Grand Center have nearly eliminated music, arts and culture from downtown and have stonewalled all attempts to reopen Kiel. They also have the Muny squeezed down to seven weeks a year. Tom Irwin moves over to Civic Progress.

Kiel Opera House is still closed.

Chapter Twenty Two

New Leaders or New Players?

September 8, 1999. Bill and Nancy Laurie announced purchase of the Blues, Kiel Center, and assumed Kiel Partner's debts. They also took control of the Opera House.

City property deals are confusing. The heirs to the Wal-Mart fortunes bought the Blues and took the lease to Kiel Center and the Opera House. The City might still own both. Or, the Lauries bought Kiel Center from Kiel Partners and control of the Opera House.

When Laurie announced his deal, he made no mention of the Opera House and told reporters he had never been in it. When asked by a reporter, Bill said they (he and Nancy) were open-minded that they'd have to get a feel from the community, and were willing to listen. (While Bill was before the microphones, his attorney Dick Thomas was *housed* at Bryan Cave *selling out* the Opera House).

Still, hopes were raised: On KMOX radio, September 8, 1999, the author expressed hope at a change in ownership. "Seems Opera House is now being viewed as an asset and he hopes Laurie would allow him to walk them through and explain his multi-use plan." The author made it clear on KMOX he did not expect the Lauries to *foot the bill*, just provide leadership.

Save the Opera House. The *Post-Dispatch* in an editorial the next day expressed hope the Lauries would help but still pointed to Kiel Partners as the responsible parties. A restored Opera House, according to the Post, would help make the European Boulevard (Market Street) one of down-town's most exciting avenues. A restored Opera House, particularly as a performance space, would add to the region's cultural mix.

But Bill and Nancy left the Opera House in the hands of Mark Sauer. Laurie's interest was to buy an NBA franchise. He was outbid in Denver, turned away in Vancouver. Laurie then said he was turning to the Blues to make them more competitive.

The Lauries liked their privacy. But they controlled Kiel Opera House at a time dozens of cities were restoring and reopening downtown theaters or opening new ones.

Bill set up his Kiel Center and St. Louis Blues Holding Company in Clayton. No City Earnings Tax. They also ripped off taxpayers by taking revenue through 'naming rights' for Kiel Center. In the fall of 2001, Paige Sports Entertainment moved downtown.

Bookend End 2007

In 2004 St. Louis celebrated the 100th anniversary of the World's Fair and the 200th anniversary of the Lewis and Clark Expedition. Only the author celebrated the 70th anniversary of the opening of Kiel Opera House. Laurie sold the Blues to Dave Checketts and his investors in 2005. At the end of 2007...

Kiel Opera House is still closed.

CHAPTER TWENTY THREE

TIF RAPE-ING ST. LOUIS

WE NEVER MET A TAX DOLLAR OR TAX BREAK WE DIDN'T LIKE

Starting with The Dome, Civic Progress and its developers began a decade-and-a half of TIF-RAPE-ING St. Louis. They also *enjoyed* some tax breaks and public assistance in destroying Kiel Auditorium and damaging and closing Kiel Opera House. By end of 2005, TIF-RAPE-ING in St. Louis has become epidemic.

Existing developers and wanna-bes: Desco, THF, McEagle, Pyramid, Steve Stogel, McGowans, etc. began throwing money at City officials in large denominations. (Missouri Ethics Commission reports since about 1996).

With newer legislation TIF-ING really took off during Francis Slay's first term. In rapid sequence, the Slay administration and the state of Missouri began throwing TIFs and/or other tax breaks at the developers on Washington Avenue, the Old Post Office, a new ballpark, and nearly $100 million in TIFs to the midtown Grand Center area.

More recently the City has been asked to fork over $38 million in TIFs for re-development of St. Louis Centre and $8 million to re-develop The Jefferson Arms.

Can a City TIF itself out? I don't know.

The tragedy? Most of these projects, particularly the Jefferson Arms on Tucker Boulevard. would have been done without TIFs, were Kiel Opera House open and marketed as the *Kennedy Center of the Midwest*. Downtown performing arts centers catalyze dramatic additional development. With Kiel delivering critical mass, filling hotels and generating tax revenue, the

City would negotiate deals from strength. The City would control these deals, not developers.

Instead the City says: *do it to me one more time.*

Bookend End 2007

When Kiel is re-opened St. Louis will have an economic catalyst/weapon with which to fight off TIFs. Until then, the City remains helpless against developers. (This is what I meant eight years ago by downtown needing one honorable deal.)

Kiel Opera House is still closed.

CHAPTER TWENTY FOUR

THE OTHER SHOE

A dozen miles west of Kiel is the St. Louis Municipal Theater in Forest Park, the largest and finest outdoor theater in America, built in the spring of 1917. In April, Mayor Henry Kiel approved the plan by the Convention Board and impresario Guy Golterman to build the theater and open with Verdi's *Aida* during the Thirteenth Annual Convention of Advertising Clubs of the World. They did and The Muny's launch was *heard* in Europe.

Muny has been a major draw to St. Louis, creating overnight stays and multiple overnight stays. St. Louis could justly label her Alone in Her Greatness.

The same consortium that has killed Kiel Opera House for a decade and a half and a few of their *friends* in Forest Park has *choked down* the Muny to seven weeks a year.

In 2001, they slipped Shakespeare Festival into Forest Park and expanded to a season beginning Memorial Day weekend through June 20th. Forest Park in June is now *free* Shakespeare below a museum — not the greatest outdoor theater in America.

August of 2003, the owners of the Fox Theater paid off the Muny Board (*Lion King* benefit) to further *choke down* The Muny. The Muny Board pretty much gutted Muny during 2004 when the great theater should have operated 100 nights.

Killing Muny costs the Theater and St. Louis 400,000–500,000 paid admissions and big travel business. UMB Bank Pavilion opens in May and operates well into October. The Fox now runs shows well into June and picks up earlier and earlier each August).

The St. Louis Sports Commission helped shut down Muny a week because 'it might need the theater for an Olympics torch ceremony'. No other St. Louis entertainment enterprise was shut down for the *movement* of the Olympics Torch through St. Louis.

Collaborating to restrain the trade of Muny and causing severe losses in entertainment-driven revenue during the tourist and vacation season are:

1. Forest Park Forever and Director Jim Mann, formerly with the Symphony

2. The Muny Board, *bowing* to grand avenue money and Civic Progress power

3. Shakespeare Festival, which knocks out Muny most of June.

4. Other Forest Park attractions who market big private-party business.

5. St. Louis City officials and Parks Department officials.

6. Metro, which is eliminating direct bus service from St. Louis County to Muny. Fox Theater Owner Harvey Harris is a Metro commissioner.

Bookend End 2007

Restraint-of-trade of Kiel Opera House and Muny to protect the Fox Theater causes an annual loss to St. Louis of $400 million in entertainment-driven revenue: on-premise-admissions, rentals, leases, food and beverage, sales and earnings tax; off premise: hotels, motels, restaurants, retail, ground and air transportation.

The travel business now goes elsewhere. The Justice Department here has been *snoozing* amid devastating violations of anti-trust laws.

Early in 2007, Frank Hamsher of Fleishman-Hillard replaced Jim Mann as President of Forest Park Forever. He was dismissed by year's end. Hamsher spent time in The Schoemehl administration. AT F-H he worked on the Civic Progress account. Forest Park Forever is Civic Progress' control mechanism in Forest Park.

Harvey Harris was replaced as a Metro Commissioner by Grand Center President Vince Schoemehl. Muny's 2008 season will again be limited and there will be no direct bus transportation to Muny from St. Louis County.

Kiel Opera House is still closed.

Mugging Kiel

Appendix

APPENDIX A.
MILESTONE EVENTS

1917

April-June. St. Louisans built and inaugurated the 11,000-seat Municipal Theater in Forest Park, first municipally-owned outdoor theater in America. It opened with Verdi's *Aida*, June 5–11, produced by impresario Guy Golterman, The Grand Opera Committee and the Ad Club Convention Board. More than 50,000 attended including delegates to the thirteenth annual convention of Ad Clubs of the World.

1919

Mayor Henry Kiel and Parks Commissioner Nelson Cunliff formed The Municipal Theater Association. The Association has presented seasons of light opera, Broadway shows, concerts and reviews ever since. 1923–1926 Golterman presented short seasons of grand opera, following the Association's productions. In 1924, a week of *Carmen* with Francesca Peralta drew 52,000, setting a new attendance mark for Muny, and garnering favorable coverage in The New York Times.

1923

St. Louisans passed an $87-million bond issue for construction of municipal buildings and public works facilities. This included $5 million for construction of the Municipal Auditorium-Convention Hall and Opera House. Mayor Kiel led the campaign. War, Prohibition and the Great Depression delayed building the civic auditorium until the early 1930s. Its fulfillment was: *Dream of a Decade.*

1932

The cornerstone was put in place on November 2nd by Mayor Victor J. Miller and Board of Public Service Director E. R. Kinsey.

1933

In April, Mayor Bernard F. Dickmann announced dedicatory events for the following spring. They would include grand opera produced by Guy Golterman. Golterman would bring stars and conductors from The Met, assemble a large St. Louis singing and dancing chorus and engage the St. Louis Symphony to comprise the Orchestra.

1934

April-June. More than 100 performances, festivals, parades, celebrations marked the opening of the Civic Auditorium on Market Street between 14th and 15th. The St. Louis Municipal Auditorium was second in size only to New York's Hippodrome, and most completely equipped. April 21st, Giovanni Martinelli and Elizabeth Rethberg of The Met starred in *Aida* to inaugurate the Opera House. Gennaro Papi conducted.

Toscanini called Rethberg: *the world's greatest soprano.* The General Director of the Met, Gatti-Casazza, described the Opera House: *with stage so magnificent as to be unsurpassed in America.* James Darst was named its first manager. Joe Killebrew provided trees from Cedar Hill, Missouri for stage sets.

October. Golterman and the Grand Opera Association presented a fall season of grand opera as *elaborate* as the April/May season. In November Zigfeld Follies filled the great stage. About this time, Kenneth Billups started the famed Legend Singers.

1930s–1980s

Kiel Opera House hosted the world's finest musicians, musical organizations, dance troupes, symphonies, Broadway-type shows and solo artists. Kiel was the *preferred* tour stop for the traveling Met. It accommodated civic events, exhibits and festivals in addition to shows and concerts.

1936–1968

Guest artists included: Marian Anderson ('58–'59) ('62–'63) Grace Bumbry, Artur Rubenstein, Van Cliburn, Piatigorsk, Rostopovitch the City was very good to the Symphony, collecting small rent and sometimes no rent, and promoting the Symphony as a civic asset.

1941

October 25. Grace Moore starred in *Tosca* in the Convention Hall, a St. Louis Grand Opera Association production.

November 28 Gennaro Papi died in New York. The premiere Puccini conductor wielded the baton for sixteen grand operas and several concerts in St. Louis.

December 7, 1941 pretty much put an end to grand opera in St. Louis until the end of WWII.

1943

The Municipal Auditorium was named Kiel Auditorium, in honor of City's first three-term mayor and builder, Henry W. Kiel. During the war, service men and women poured into Kiel for shows, concerts and U.S.O. dances. It is two blocks east of Union Station.

The Opera House was home for the St. Louis Symphony. Conductors included Vladamir Golschmann, Eduardo Van Ramourtel and Elezar de Carvallo.

1946

May 7-8. St. Louis Light Opera Guild presented *Student Prince* with New York tenor, Donald Gage, St. Louis soprano Maria Marceno, Marion Marlowe, and Emil Wachter. Kenneth Schuller was musical director.

May 13-15. The MET returned to St. Louis for first time in 30 years. 30,000 attend performances in Convention Hall. Traubel and Thornborg in *Tannheuser*; Rise Stevens, Albanese and Hugh Thompson in *Carmen*; Warren, Peerce, Munsel and Pinza in *Rigoletto*.

1947

March 12. Grace Moore cancels Golterman-arranged concert in the Convention Hall because of her husband's illness. The Met's Cesare Sodero was to conduct 80 St. Louis musicians. The Light Opera Guild presented a second season.

1949

Charles Dewitt's concessions contract at Kiel Auditorium is declared invalid (Charlie got caught up in a change of administrations).

1951

January 2. City sponsors free Symphony concert to promote the Symphony.

December 10. William Warfield, bass-baritone, appeared in concert in the Opera House.

December 18. Globe-Democrat Christmas Chorale Pageant.

5/27/49, 2/5/56, 2/1/64, 11/29/53, 2/18/55, 2/16/55, 1/20/56, 1/21/56. Ken Billups and Legend Singers, Ken Billups and the Sumner High School Choir

1950s—1980s

Among the stars who performed in Kiel Opera House: Duke Ellington, Count Basie, Ella Fitzgerald, Louie Armstrong, Bob Hope, Carol Channing, Katherine Hepburn, The Rat Pack, Diana Ross and the Supremes, Elvis Presley, Johnny Cash, Danny Thomas, Neil Diamond, Guy Lombardo, Red Foxx, Paul Anka, Mary Martin, Tony Bennett, Ray Charles, Eddie Arnold, Bette Midler, Perry Como, Jack Benny, Judy Garland, Benny Goodman and his Orchestra, Steve Lawrence and Edie Gorme, Fred Waring Chorale, Liberace, Hank Williams, Sr. and Jr.

Broadway Touring Shows included: *South Pacific, King and I, Coco, Unsinkable Molly Brown, Best Little Whorehouse, My Fair Lady* with Rex Harrison; Carol Channing in *Hello, Dolly*; Yul Brenner in *King and I; The Wiz, A Chorus Line,* and *Hair.*

1950s

The Opera House enjoyed a solid schedule of traveling shows, concerts, civic events, graduations and celebrations. During this decade, Muny Opera auditions were held in assembly halls, finals in the Opera House.

1951

January 25. St. Louis Symphony presented a free concert, subsidized by the City.

1952

Metropolitan Opera presented *Aida, Carmen, Boheme,* and *La Traviata.*

December 22. The Third Annual Globe-Democrat Christmas Chorale Pageant in the Convention Hall drew 12,000. Grace Bumbry performed with St. Louis Symphony.

1954

April. Globe-Democrat presented the National Folk Festival-cultural performances and exhibits. Pete Seeger's first appeared in St. Louis in Kiel Opera House.

1965

June 20. The Rat Pack: Frank Sinatra, Dean Martin, Sammy Davis Jr. and Johnny Carson headlined the Teamsters-arranged benefit for Dismas House. The concert, which was closed-circuited to New York and Chicago, raised $300,000.

1980s

Dance St. Louis brought the Joffrey Ballet, Alvin Ailey, Paul Taylor, Kansas City Ballet and Merce Cunningham. Opera House is neglected, pressures build from midtown to close her or just let her die.

1984

Former Alderman Bruce Sommer, manager of Kiel Auditorium, is also appointed manager of Cervantes Convention Center. Would one or both suffer? *Caretaker* attitude replaces *marketing* attitude. Two theater/auditoriums were turned into courts and offices.

1985

January 27. Post-Dispatch (Charlene Prost) 'It never had anyone to **sell** it, if it had a good marketing staff, it could be creating its own events and bringing even more new business to the City'. Arena owner Harry Ornest said Kiel didn't represent competition. Ornest spent **2.5** million upgrading the Arena on Oakland Avenue.

Friends of Kiel raises funds to restore Kiel. Glenn Sheffield heads the effort. Manager Bruce Sommer: 'With Kiel's Opera House, four smaller theaters and 140 dressing rooms, it could become one of the *premiere* entertainment centers in the area' — just needs to be *marketed.*

January 29. Ron Elz' column in The Post-Dispatch commented on Golterman's gathering of historical material. Author receives calls for interviews.

October 10. Kenneth Brown Billups dies at age 67 during a Legend Singers rehearsal. He was one of St. Louis' music *giants.*

November 7. Author wrote Sommer, Sheffield, Mary Hendron, America's Center; Jack Keane-Mayor's Office; and Joe Bergfeld, St. Louis Ambassadors; offering to help develop fund raisers based on *share your memories* audio and visual exhibit.

Golterman gathered 20 hours of interviews on tape. No response.

1990s

1990

July 7. Kiel Center Redevelopment Corporation was formed as a Missouri company. Directors were: M. Edwin Trusheim, CEO General American Life; Lee M. Liberman, CEO Laclede Gas; and Ted C. Wetterau, CEO, Wetterau Inc.; all Civic Progress. Legal Counsel: Bryan Cave (Walter Metcalfe, Jr.) PR Firm: Fleishman-Hillard.

December 27. St. Louis Aldermen approve plan calling for tearing down Convention Hall, replacing it with an 18,500 seat arena; renovating / re-opening the Opera House and operating the center as a **civic-events**, entertainment and sports facility. Agreement is between the City of St. Louis (Land Clearance for Redevelopment Authority) and Kiel Center Redevelopment Corp. Kiel Partner's attorneys are Grand Center's attorneys.

Assaults on the Opera House begin.

1991

May 4. Final performance in Opera House-St. Louis Philharmonic-*take your Chairs*. They did. The Opera House is closed. Mark Sauer, President of Kiel Center says the new arena and the Opera House **will** re-open in 1994. *Friends of Kiel* disband.

Kiel Opera House was closed for upgrading on May 7, 1991.

1992

November 10. City takes responsibility for site preparation costs, building and operating a parking garage with City getting the revenue. Representing Kiel Center Redevelopment is Bryan Cave (Walter Metcalfe, Jr.) Judson W. Perkins is the new President of Kiel Center Redevelopment Corp., Alfred H. Kerth III, Secretary. City commitment is about $35 million. Kiel Partners spent $137 million. Destruction begins.

November. Kiel Partners and City sign lease that will destroy the Convention Hall to build a hockey arena for the Blues and to build a parking garage. The clear understanding is that the deal will also upgrade and reopen the Opera House.

December 9. Kiel Partners insists the Arena be prevented from presenting *for-admission* events. This *no compete* clause eventually killed the Arena.

1994

May 12. Kiel Center President Judd Perkins to author: "*Re-opening of the Opera House will occur sometime in 1995. Renovation of the mechanical systems is underway with aesthetic refurbishment's currently being studied by our architect.*"

October 8. Kiel Center opens with an exhibition professional basketball game, followed by a Frank Sinatra concert. The Opera House remained sealed off and closed.

November 15. Kiel Partners cease work on the Opera House and dismiss the prime contractor. The City produces a *certificate of completion* relieving Kiel Partners of any further obligation. $2.5 million had been spent on the Opera House-side. Most went to repairing damage, removing asbestos and sealing it off from the other side.

1995

January 26. St. Louis Blues play their first home game in Kiel Center.

February 10. Kiel Partner's Al Kerth, III said the opening of the Opera House would be delayed, but that it would be opened as soon as possible.

June. Blues' Chairman Mike Shanahan is replaced by Jerry Ritter, former Anheuser-Busch executive. Mike Keenan is named Coach and General Manager. Jack Quinn remains President of the Blues.

October 28th Ward Alderman Dan McGuire calls for investigation, urges City to consider suing Kiel Partners toward completion of restoration of the Opera House.

1996

January 19. Aldermen adopt Associate City Counselor Fran Oates' opinion that Kiel Partners and Land Clearance for Redevelopment Authority had an *obligation* to restore Opera House. After heated discussion, Board of Aldermen and Board of Estimate decide **not** to pursue Kiel Partners on the matter.

They accept the *certificate of completion* as the **guiding** document. What were the pressures-threats or payoffs? Was the certificate keep concealed? Was it a newer document-post-dated? *Their lawyers are better than ours.* Cries to *sue 'em* rang out. However, *them* are Civic Progress.

Fox Associates (Fox Theater) conducted a *study*, and called for the Opera House exterior to be preserved and the inside **gutted**, and used for **parking.**

Civic Progress/Kiel Partners spokesmen voice a consistent message: Kiel Partners never promised to re-open the Opera House. If the city pursued legal action it risks offending Civic Progress, and jeopardizing support for future projects.)

December 19. Jerry Ritter fires Jack Quinn and Larry Keenan, brings back Mark Sauer as President, Joel Quenneville is named coach, Larry Pleau, general manager

1997

Mayor Clarence Harmon launches Downtown Plan. Comptroller Darlene Green seeks some *course* for the Opera House. Pressures from Grand Center and Kiel Partners increase-to keep it closed, destroy it, or turn it into something else. Alderman McGuire becomes Parks Director. San Francisco completes renovation of its earthquake-damaged War Memorial Opera House. The work was completed in eighteen months and cost $88 million. They celebrated the 75th season of the San Francisco Grand Opera.

1998

The Assaults. The Defense. This year is thoroughly covered in early chapters.

February–March. Three studies are undertaken with the common objective to gut the Opera House main theater to *protect* the Fox Theater and Kiel Center: the ULI Study, the 2004 Study and the Smithsonian Study.

Ed Golterman, H. Russell Carter, Jeff and Elle Stewart started working against these efforts. *This is dirty business.*

April. Support to save and re-open the Opera House builds. Golterman, the Stewarts, Russ Carter and St. Louis Core's Gary Bill re-awaken St. Louisans to the value of Kiel Opera House and defend it against its would-be destroyers. They formed Kiel for Performing Arts and assembled a board. *Intermission* magazine begin covering the effort along with Core, then other publications and radio and TV stations came aboard.

June. Opera Theater (Webster Groves) buys the old Selkirk auction house for *storage and rehearsal space,* according to Charles MacKay, General Director. The building is on Olive Street west of Grand Center. Danforth Foundation declines to help reopen the Opera House. Bruce Anderson: *we fund 'projects directly affixed to Downtown Now Plan'.* D.F. spent at least $100,000 on the Smithsonian Study.

July 1. Maureen McAvey abruptly resigns as Director of the St. Louis Development Corporation, ending a three-year stay in St. Louis. She and Mark Sauer co-chaired Urban Land Institute Study. She fled before the culmination of the ULI study.

July 4. Golterman writes document supporting re-opening Kiel Opera House as a multi-use civic center, including the main theater. He forwards document to the ULI Panel coming to St. Louis later in the month.

July 8. Mark Sauer verbally assaults Golterman following a ULI task force meeting in a Kiel Center conference room. K-FPA holds fund-raisers, petition drives, obtains an aldermanic resolution, captures more media coverage, submits business plans and builds a professional team to restore and reopen the Opera House.

November. K-FPA's Golterman, Carter, William Neal, the Stewarts have a lease developed by attorney Alan Steinberg. (A lease must be ready when and if seed money or other financing came into place). The lease called for restoring and re-opening the Opera House as a civic center, primarily with private investment and endowments, and sharing income and revenues with the city.

November–December. K-FPA officers take potential investors, and officials of several performing groups through the Opera House, including Evan Schwartzfarb, Palm Capital; John Kinnamon, Burn Brae Dinner Theater; investment broker, Joe Dubuque; and New Theater's Agnes Wilcox.

December. Kiel Partners (Clark Enterprises) cover the Blues' operating losses for the fourth time this year, $17.7 million. Total cash calls over four years is nearly $70 million.

December 2. First K-FPA fund raiser is a concert at Windows on Washington. Despite a heavy snow storm 250 attended.

1999

January 19. John Danforth refers author to St. Louis 2004 arts facilities study **by** *top professionals in the field.* (A month earlier the Post editorialized that *focusing on Grand Center as the city struggles to revitalize downtown is shortsighted*).

February 27. The Arena is imploded- a *media* event with fireworks, music and news helicopters. It came down. The Kiel deal not only destroyed Kiel Auditorium, damaged and wasted the Opera House but it also destroyed The Arena.

City officials continue to be closed-minded to Opera House proposals. They impose impossible demands on potential developers, preservationists.

May 26. Developer Sam Glaser offered to buy the Opera House for $1 million, raise additional cash, restore and re-open it as a civic performing and arts center. Comptroller Green: *the City didn't take it seriously.* Three months later she gives it away for $1 a year.

September 6. Bill and Nancy Laurie (Wal-Mart) announce purchase of the Blues and Kiel Center, and gain control of the Opera House. Hopes rise that new Lease holders would see the value in the Opera House and help re-open it.

September 7. K-FPA Chairman Ed Golterman on KMOX-Radio: *"I'm encouraged. Laurie is a competitor. Let the Opera House compete. The Blues and Kiel*

Center are civic assets, so too is the Opera House'. Golterman asked to take The Lauries through. He was denied.

Attorney Dick Thomas is put in charge of Kiel Center and the Blues.

He sets up office at Bryan Cave-Civic Progress/Kiel Partners/Danforth/ Metcalfe).

September 25. K-FPA volunteers string 150 feet of petitions-sheets from Bear-to-Bear in front of Kiel Opera House-nearly 4,700 signatures.

October 8-11 Golterman goes to Washington D.C. to clarify The Smithsonian's involvement in Kiel Opera House. *None,* according to Michael Carrigan and Mary Tanner. Conversion would be cost-prohibitive. This is not what St. Louisans have been told. Phil Dine of the Post's Washington Bureau told St. Louisans *The Smithsonian was not interested in Kiel Opera House.*

October. Glennon Company strengthens business/marketing plan for K-FPA.

Sunday, November. 7. KMOV-TV's Imagine St. Louis and spread in P-D. lets St. Louisans see the beauty of the Opera House. Golterman appeared on the program. The Kiel advocate called for the City to announce before the end of the year that the Opera House would be reopened. He called on The Lauries to lead, pointed to the Opera House as good business. Ellen Futterman of the Post-Dispatch suggested another *study.*

Sunday, November 14. P-D publishes fifteen support letters in its Imagine St. Louis section. Golterman assembled a collage of the letters and color pictures of the interior.

November–December. The Lauries decline to let K-FPA team present business plan and take the them through. Bill and Nancy took the Mark Sauer tour.

November 24. News Release–Author challenges Sauer and David Fay (the Fox) to a round of boxing each at the Guns and Hoses charity boxing show at Kiel Center. And, called them bastards. His access to the Opera House ends.

December. K-FPA-Inc. Joan Caro and Burt Holtzman obtain/decorate tree for the Festival of Trees. More sign petitions. Golterman goes to Nashville to see The Tennessee Performing Arts Center. He has Imagine St. Louis TV program duplicated and sent to City officials and business leaders.

December 20. Golterman submits Kiel Opera House to National Trust for Historic Preservation for consideration as One of *Eleven Most Endangered Historic Places.*

December. Golterman breaks with K-FPA board over differences in the mission. The Board criticized him for aggressiveness, Golterman said The Board was losing courage. He held a Millennium eve vigil outside the Opera House.

2000

January 4. EG, Tom Klein, Windows on Washington, Marilyn Stanza

St. Louis Ballet Co.; and Glen Jamboretz, Glennon Co. call on Post-Dispatch's editorial board represented by Sue Hegger and Charlene Prost. The group presented

Their latest business plan and called on the Post for leadership. The Post never acknowledged the meeting, receiving the materials, nor did it report on the meeting.

Friday, January 21. In Aldermanic debate of the City's cable access options, Steve Conway laments *how clauses and agreements that restrict competition hurt the City.* He referred to the Kiel Partners deal and The Arena. The Cardinals' push for a new stadium dominates the news.

February 4. Windows on Washington hosted the *Business Journal's* 40-under 40-Awards. Cardinals' President Mark Lamping *hawks* plan for a new base-ball stadium. He calls on taxpayers to help pay for it. Asks: *why should he help Golterman with Opera House?*

February 17. Golterman sends Financing Plan to Mark Sauer. No response.

February–March. Letters are heavily against public funding for new stadium. A KMOX Radio (informal) poll showed heavy opposition to using tax money for a new ballpark.

March and April. March 3rd Golterman sent latest version of business plan for Kiel Opera House to *Riverfront Times.* Proposed new stadium is in the news, nothing on Opera House. Downtown Now pushes state lawmakers to allow City and County voters to ballot on a tax increase for 'infrastructure work'.

April 25. Author goes to Jefferson City to see what stalls lawmakers' support of the Downtown Now plan. Legislators felt pushed, they were not given enough information and that the plan was vague.

May. St. Louis University forms committee to study building a basketball arena on campus—estimated cost—$50 million. Jefferson City says neither tax money nor tax breaks would be approved for the Cardinals or Blues. State lawmakers tabled the bill to allow a tax referendum to cover infrastructure costs for a new ballpark.

June. Bill Laurie remains silent on the Opera House, announces new sound system for Kiel Center and removal of 400 seats for lounge/food/beverage facility.

June 26. Post-Dispatch Imagine Section–On Downtown Now Plan (no Opera House) (Kiel Center books 200+ events a year. The Opera House remains closed, sealed off). City Hall-silent. K-FPA-silent. Lauries-silent. Opera House is off the radar screen.

June 15-July 4. Golterman begins manuscript, asks Justice Department to investigate the Kiel deals and the stonewalling of its reopening.

Chancellor Touhill, University of Missouri-St. Louis, sees *no conflict* between a performing arts center on campus and a re-opened Kiel Opera House. UMSL would partner with Kiel on educational programs/performances.

August. Fox Theater owner Harvey Harris is named Chairman of the board of public television station KETC. Channel 9 is in Grand Center.

August 28. Bill Laurie announces sale of Kiel Center name to Savvis for $70 million.

September The Lauries complete the sale. Mayor Harmon won't go after some of the money for the people of St. Louis, because he was *afraid the City would lose a suit.*

September.12. Blue's President Mark Sauer points to $20 million a year deficit–Blues and Savvis Center. Owners will go back to Jefferson City for tax *help* for maintenance.

September 14. The Post-Dispatch reports the City of St. Louis lost 15.8% of its population during the last decade of the 20th century, largest % loss of any city in the U.S. Same issue of the Post ran a photo of the L (of Kiel) coming down from Kiel Center.

October 10. Post-Dispatch reported Kiel family was invited to Blues' opening hockey game and given a picture of Kiel/Savvis Center.

October 19. On KMOX — Tina Sinatra tells hosts Brennan and Millhaven *'it was the highlight of her life'* when her father brought her on the stage at the Rat Pack concert.

October 28–November 1. Golterman walks from the Opera House to Columbia, Missouri. Bill Laurie declined to meet with him. Ed leaves material urging re-opening of the Opera House including substantial *naming* potential and a 222-page history of the last ten years.

November 5. Paige Sports' Dick Thomas writes E.G: *The Lauries are not interested in investing huge sums of money in the Opera House.* Golterman reminds Thomas he and his group asked the Lauries only for leadership.

December. Cardinals want public funding and/or tax relief for a new ballpark. Golterman submits Kiel to the National Trust as one of *the Eleven Most Endangered.* He calls on The St. Louis Bar Association to investigate attorneys Metcalfe, Arnold, Harris and Bornstein, and offers to debate them at St. Louis University Law School.

Downtown St. Louis has been rendered *non-competitive* in conventions, tourism, and cultural/ entertainment by restrictive covenants and restraint of trade. Evidence:

1996 **Detroit** opened its Opera House-a renovated downtown 1920s movie palace

1996 **Chicago** completed $100 million restoration of Civic Opera House-built 1929

1997 **San Francisco** Opera celebrated its 75th season, in renovated War Memorial

1998 **Seattle** opened Benaroya Hall, two-venue concert and performance center

1998 **Cleveland** opened the Allen Theater, the fourth in downtown's Playhouse Square

1999 **Pittsburgh** opened two more theaters for live production downtown, now offers five

1999 **Nashville** hosted the regional Met Auditions in its downtown performing arts

1999 **Chicago** opened Shakespeare Theater on Navy Pier

2000 **Chicago** re-opened renovated Goodman Theater
2000 **New York** re-opened a 778 Theater built in 1918, renovated for $25 million

2000 **Memphis** is building a theater/concert hall downtown, near Convention Center

2001 **New Jersey** Performing Arts Center credited with revitalizing downtown Newark

2001

April. SFX looks at Opera House. Sauer says don't raise hopes. Former Mayor Schoemehl is appointed President of Grand Center. Mayor Slay loads up his administration with ex-Schoemehl staffers and consultants.

May. Opera House has been closed ten years. State Legislature approves tax funding for a new basketball arena at MO. U. after Bill Laurie offered $25 million, then threatened to withdraw it if the legislature did not approve public funding. Laurie has offered neither money nor leadership to reopen Kiel. His hockey team failed to reach the Stanley Cup finals and he lost lots of money, or wrote off lots of loses.

June. City, State and County are poised to throw tax dollars/breaks at the Cardinals for a replacement ballpark and Cardinals Village-all behind closed doors. Golterman forms group to put at plaque on the Kiel Opera House. National Trust did not include Kiel Opera House on Eleven Most Endangered list. Grand Center's Schoemehl (P-D, J Berger) suggests Opera House be used as a museum of U.S. Grant.

July. Channel 9 has become a 'commercial' station for grand center, linking spots or commercials promoting its real estate projects and entertainment venues. Ted Garcia has moved out West and Mike Hardgrove retired. Emily Pulitzer's Museum in grand center is about to open. Laurie gets his basketball arena in Columbia. Gov. Holden commits $35 million. Coalition Against Public Funding for ballpark starts petition drive. Sheraton-City Center opens, one block south of the Opera House.

Blues officials ask the City to lobby the state for tax money for Savvis. Slay said no. Petition drive against public funding for a new ballpark falls 1,000 short.

Requests to the State for public funding for sports facilities could reach three quarters of a billion dollars — St. Louis, Kansas City, Springfield, MO University. Author asks P-D to find out if The Lauries signed an agreement to keep Opera House closed.

September. Stages deal in Kirkwood falls through. EG suggests Stages as a major tenant in Kiel Opera House-bring seniors downtown. (Seniors comprise 70% of their audience.)

Clear Channel negotiates with City to take over, re-store and re-open it as a theater.

Clear Channel is talking with Dance St. Louis and Stages as possible 'users' of the Opera House. Cash-strapped State gives Missouri U. $35 million for a basketball arena.

October. Golterman raises $700 for Opera House plaque. 254 give $1.00 to help purchase.

November. Plaque is ordered. Channel 11 does a feature, interviewing Mayor Slay and Ed Golterman.

December. EG asks St. Louis County to become strong public partner in Opera House Re-opening. Is SFX scared off by 'the poor economy' or by Grand Center. Kiel Man holds December 31 vigil at Opera House-closed ten years.

2002

January. Mayor Slay *rides* the new ballpark *horse* hard. Schoemehl builds an *empire* on Grand Avenue. St. Louis loses $6 million a year tax revenue x multiplier. Opera House market: 2.6 million residents of the region, another 20 million in seven contiguous states who would find it easier to come to St. Louis, than to other cities for theater.

Downtown is not competitive for year 'round tourism. MetroLink stop is a block away. Fox Theater owner Harvey Harris and Alberici's Bob McCoole reveal a plan to *gut the main theater* of Kiel Opera House and turn it into a school for performing arts. They will seek $70 million, primarily public money. Sauer said Lauries would like to help.

P-D runs a mild support editorial. Ed Golterman *travels* Opera House exhibit-April, 1934-1991, gathers 10,000 signatures. Al Kerth dies-eulogized as a civic leader.

September. Savvis Center *drapes* off the hockey arena to create a 4,000-seat concert space. One of the finest concert halls in America is a few yards away. Harvey Harris calls the Opera House a *relic.* It is six years younger than the Fox.

Grand Center receives $80 million in TIFs for two dozen+ projects including a basketball arena for SLU and an African American Museum. Was there a hearing? Golterman urges City residents to vote before public money would be used to gut Opera House.

Board of Aldermen is asked to quickly approve public funds for a new ballpark to "take advantage of preferred bond interest rates. (eleven years ago Kiel Partners/Civic Progress rammed through the Kiel deal with the same pressure, launching the most destructive deal in City history.) Cardinals say they are considering locations other than downtown.

Aldermanic action denies St. Louisans a chance to vote on the issue.

Golterman again asks Justice Dept., US Attorney for Eastern MO., MO Attorney General and St. Louis Circuit Attorney to investigate the Kiel deals. Start with the lawyers.

Focus on Bryan Cave's Walter Metcalfe, Jr. and Linda Martinez (Grand Center and Civic Progress/Kiel Partners); and Fox Theater owner, Harvey Harris-Stolar Partnership.

October 2. P-D reports School Superintendent. Cleveland Hammons prefers a m midtown location for a performing arts school, not Kiel Opera House.

October 7. Golterman calls on Slay to remove former Schoemehl staffers from Convention and Visitors Commission. *Put people on Commission who will improve downtown.*

November 6. P-D reports St. Louis school board has received plan by Harris and McCoole to *gut* Kiel Opera House. Same day, RFT reports Grand Center President Vince Schoemehl is considering putting together a slate of candidates for school board.

December 1. St. Louis University Board Chairman and Grand Center Chairman J. Joe Adjoran calls for Clear Channel to build a theater in Grand Center and to come together to (gut Kiel Opera House) EG demands to address SLU Board and calls New Year's eve vigil.

2003

January-March. Grand Center attempts to take over School Board by having CEO Vince Schoemehl and Bob Archibald, Pres. of the Missouri Historical Society run for the Board. The grand center slate is described as the 'mayor's' slate. Gain quick control, gut the Opera House main theater, give the owners of the Fox their prize.

Danforth and Civic Progress back the Grand Center school board slate. Superintendent Hammonds announces his retirement. Another museum is planned for midtown -Black History Museum. Public television station KETC continues to sponsor and promote attractions at the privately-owned Fox Theater, the latest is an appearance by The Irish Tenors. Author tours exhibit to keep Kiel *before* the people.

April 15. Grand Center slate wins control of St. Louis School Board. John Danforth announces Foundation money will fund life sciences and biotech projects. He *gives up* on downtown after spending millions to give St. Louis a lackluster 2004.

May 9. Developer Don Breckenridge announces he will restore and re-open Kiel Opera House. Clear Channel Entertainment and Fox Associates would help split bookings. Kiel Opera House goes to its *enemies.*

June-July. The latest Kiel *deal cooks* behind closed doors. They will miss The 70th Anniversary of its opening–April 1934.

Breckenridge refuses offers from Golterman to help pre-market the Opera House. Author took the Kiel exhibit to the Adam's Mark for Fair St. Louis and to The Millenium Hotel for Sister Cities International Convention. Breckenridge asks media to give him a *free ride* for a few months.

August-December. Ed G travels Kiel exhibit, plans to honor the Opera House during 2004-The 70th Anniversary of its opening. He will hold another New Years Eve vigil.

December 2. St. Louis County Council commits $45 million toward The Cardinal's *replacement* ballpark. The County is on the *hook* to repay principal and interest on the bonds which is $110 million over 30 years. Money will come from hotel/motel taxes.

December 18. Cardinal's owners and City officials break ground on replacement ballpark.

2004

January-March Nothing. Project seems stalled around the phony parking *issue.* News media lowers another blanket of silence over Kiel.

April May June. Golterman submits alternate plans for parking, urges Metropolis, Junior League, Civic Progress, City Hall, RCGA, and the SLCVC to get involved.

July August September. A consultant to The RCGA, pocketed 1.4 million. He claimed to be clairvoyant. David Levin was dismissed only after his claims were published in a British magazine. Bureaucrats and consultants line their pockets.

July 26. Page 14. Newsweek describes how restored theaters and opera houses sparked downtown rebirths. Golterman has called for the firing of Dick Fleming, consolidating RCGA and SLCVC, and moving them out of the high rent – One Metropolitan Square.

St. Louis County Council approves another $200,000 for the RCGA for *economic development*. The RCGA hires another consultant, this one from Kansas City, as a high paid V-P Pinnacle Entertainment is given state gaming commission approval for casinos in Lemay and in downtown St. Louis.

The author hears from organizations seeking to *book* Kiel Opera House for performances and events. He refers them to Breckenridge.

September. Golterman asks organized labor to break the logjam-$10 million for the Richard Gephardt Theater in Kiel Opera House, honoring the Congressman on his retirement. Gephardt has been a long-time support of organized labor and its causes. And, he started his political career as a St. Louis alderman, a block from Kiel.

2005

Pulitzer Publishing is sold to Lee Enterprises of Davenport, Iowa—loss of another corporate headquarters. May Companies are sold to Federated-loss of another corporate headquarters. Kiel Opera House is stonewalled another year.

Author offers to re-open her for a consortium of owners of the downtown hotels and motels and to vigorously market hotel/show weekend *packages*.

Don Breckenridge dies from the effects of cancer on November 30. In May of 2003, he announced he would renovate and reopen Kiel Opera House. He did neither.

2006

Dave Checketts and investors buy The St. Louis Blues and take the lease to Savvis Center and Kiel Opera House. From January 1, 2006 to September 1, 2006 there was not one word from Checketts, his investors, or his staff regarding Kiel Opera House

Sunday, August 20. Post-Dispatch runs article on the dramatic decline in tourism and conventions citing a substantial decline in attendance at the Gateway Arch.

January-July. Author submits: conventions, travel groups and those who travel for entertainment chose cities with downtown performing arts and other big downtown cultural and entertainment attractions. St. Louis comes up very short.

Springfield Il. offers The Lincoln Museum and Library and a downtown performing arts center, The Hoagland.

Breckenridge/Clear Channel signs have been taken down from in front of Kiel. 2006 ends with one of the two flagpoles broken off, trash and urine littering its entrances; bedding, cracked stonework and concrete gracing the front and 14th street side. The Renaissance Grand *convention* hotel can not make interest payments on its loans. St. Louis region has lost 33,000 jobs against moderate to strong job increases in 300 regions throughout The U.S.

2007

January. St. Louis Business Journal ran a front-page article describing Dave Checkett's plan to restore and reopen Kiel Opera House. Indications were work would begin before the end of 2007. Mayor Slay, Development Director Geisman and The Mayor's Chief of Staff, Jeff Rainford had no comment.

By September, Slay was pushing for an outdoor stage on The Memorial Plaza across from City Hall and more artwork on the Gateway Mall east of Tucker. The Business Journal reported in early September that the rate for filling downtown lofts, condos, and apartments has fallen quite a bit behind the rate of construction.

November December. St. Louis Business Journal reports City officials (Slay, Rainford, Geisman) seek $100 million in new markets tax credits for Centene to lure them to Ballpark Village. In December Pinnacle opened its Lumiere Casino downtown.

By the end of 2007 over half-a-billion dollars in public funding and/or TIFS have been committed by public officials for the replacement ballpark, ballpark village and Centene. The year ends with Ballpark Village deal seriously stalled, the Bottle District-stalled and still *no comment* on Kiel Opera House from City Hall. Whatever is or is not happening is happening behind closed doors and Grand Center celebrates another year of keeping Kiel Opera House closed. The *Fix* is still in.

APPENDIX B.
PERFORMANCES

Grand Opera opened the Coliseum at Washington and Jefferson (1910), the Municipal Theater in Forest Park (1917), and the Opera House (1934). Guy Golterman's grand operas in the Opera House and Convention Hall.

April 21, 1934 *Aida*–Elizabeth Rethberg and Giovanni Martinelli Opera House

April 23, 1934 *Il Trovatore*–Rethberg and Martinelli Opera House

April 25, 1934 *Cavalleria–Rusticana and Pagliacci* Opera House

April 28, 1934 *Butterfly*–Lucrecia Bori and Mario Chamlee Opera House

May. 5, 1934 *Boheme*–Lucrecia Bori and Mario Chamlee Opera House

October 8, 1934 *La Rondine*–Lucrecia Bori and Mario Chamlee Opera House

October 10, 1934 *Carmen*–Martinelli Cloe Glade Lucy Monroe Opera House

October 13, 1934 *Madame Butterfly*–Paggi Chamlee Gandolfi Opera House

October 15, 1934 *La Boheme* Opera House

October 20, 1934 *Lohengrin*–Sellout Rethberg and Chamlee Opera House

October 22, 1934 *Tosca*–Sellout Maria Jeritza Mario Chamlee Opera House

October 26, 1934 *Andrea Chenier*–Martinelli and Rethberg Opera House

December 25–January 15 Reinhardt's–*A Midsummer Night's Dream* Opera House

February 18, 1935 Ted Shaw and His Dancers Opera House

Fortune Gallo's *San Carlo* Opera of Boston and Philadelphia
Guy Golterman Producer/Director

April 22, 1935 *Madame Butterfly* Opera House
April 23, 1935 *Aida* Opera House
April 24, 1935 *Lohengrin* Opera House
April 25, 1935 *Cavalleria Rusticana and Pagliacci* Opera House
April 26, 1935 *Rigoletto* Opera House
April 27, 1935 *Martha* and *San Carlo Ballet* Opera House
April 27, 1935 *Il Trovatore* Opera House

St. Louis Grand Opera Company–Guy Golterman, Director:

October 31, 1935 *Turandot,* Jeritza, Vettori and Bentonelli Convention Hall
November 2, 1935 *Tristan and Isolde*–Althouse and Halstead Convention Hall
November 4, 1935 *Tännhauser*–Maria Jeritza and Paul Althouse
Convention Hall
November 6, 1935 *Faust*–Martinelli Rothier Monroe Convention Hall

San Carlo Productions (January 5, 6, 7, 8 1936) Opera House

St. Louis Opera Company–Guy Golterman, Director Spring, 1936 Season:
April 16, 1936 *La Traviata*–Edith Mason, Mario Chamlee Opera House
April 18, 1936 Opera Ball and Concert Opera House
April 20, 1936 *Lucia* with Lily Pons and Joseph Bentonelli 9,700+ sets
indoor record. (Caruso and Metropolitan Opera at the St. Louis Coliseum,
1910 drew 9000+) Miss Pons was called back nine times after her Mad
Scene aria Convention Hall
April 22, 1936 *La Gioconda*–Rosa Raisa Mario Chamlee Opera House
December 2, 1936 Lily Pons in Concert Convention Hall
March 41, 1937 Mrs. Martin Johnson–Lecture Opera House
March 16, 1937 Betty Jaynes–Chicago Opera Co. Concert Opera House

St. Louis Opera Company–Guy Golterman, Director

November 22, 1937 *Barber of Seville* Erna Sack Claudio Frigerio Opera House
November 24, 1937 *Carmen Martinelli* Bruna Castangna Weede Opera House
December 1, 1937 *Tristan und Isolde* Flagstad Althouse Opera House

March 12, 1937 Guy Golterman and Guy Jr. attend Metropolitan Opera's production of *La Boheme* in New York with Martinelli as Rodolfo. Papi conducted.

April 23, 1938 *Opera Gala* Martinelli Weede, Marceno, Gurney, De LePorte and Ballet

April 25, 1938 *Opera Gala* Same Performers, Different Program Maestro Gennaro Papi, who conducted without a score, conducted most all of the Puccini works in the Kiel Opera House and a total of sixteen performances for Golterman.

Golterman worked from an office in the Jefferson Hotel. He often missed his productions because he was working on future productions. As his health failed in 1938, he probably knew grand opera would not last as a popular art form in St. Louis.But, for 30-plus years he gave St. Louis the best–Caruso and Gluck in The Coliseum; Peralta and Salazar at Muny; Martinelli, Rethberg and Pons at Kiel.

Golterman brought famed dance companies to St. Louis including the Royal Russian Ballet with Pavolva; the London Symphony, and individual artists such as John McCormack and Chicago's Mary Garden. Golterman's grand operas paid 80+ percent of costs through ticket sales and program advertising. Shipping sets from Chicago hurt, financially, as did cancellations by Grace Moore and Chaliapin.

In 1938 the St. Louis Grand Opera Association replaced Golterman, naming Laszlo Halasz-Director and Walter Head-Chairman of the Board. Halasz told them he could get the stars *cheaper*. They would pattern their *operation* after the Municipal Theater in Forest Park. Their productions never came close to Golterman's in quality or style.

St. Louis Grand Opera Association productions in the Municipal Auditorium:

April 17, 1939 *Walkure* Lauritz Melchior Marjorie Lawrence Opera House

April 21, 1939 *Othello* Giovanni Martinelli Irene Jessner Opera House

April 24, 1939 *Faust* Charles Kullman Pinza Lucy Monroe Opera House

October 14, 1939 *Aida*

October 21, *Boheme*

November 14, *Amelia and Pagliacci* Convention Hall

November 14, 1939 Ernest Lert resigned as stage director in a dispute with Halasz.

April 1940 *Manon, Rigoletto, Carmen*. 1941 *October Martha, Tosca Falstaff.*

The Bach Society and St. Louis Philharmonic performed at Kiel. Marion Anderson appeared in concert February 1, 1940; January 28, 1941. The Metropolitan Opera touring Company placed Kiel Opera House and St. Louis in the top five cities on its tours during the 1950s and 60s. Fausto Cleva conducted here frequently. John Vickers, Lucia Albanase, Mario Del Monico, and Franco Corelli were among the stars appearing in St. Louis. (Producers said the Opera House was the *best* house in the country).

The big stage accommodated large sets, full chorus, principals and dancers. The rising orchestra pit held 70 musicians. Acoustics were so good the orchestra did not need amplification. The St. Louis Light Opera Guild presented *The Student Prince,* May 7–8, 1946 with Donald Gage (New York), Maria Marceno Golterman and Marian Townsend (Marian Marlowe).

1946–1947. Golterman *booked* American soprano/international star, Grace Moore, and Metropolitan Opera conductor Cesare Sodero. Miss Moore cancelled her March 27 appearance due to her husband's severe illness. They rescheduled for July 1947 but she died in a plane crash at Copenhagen in January.

Elvis, Van Cliburn, Victor Borge, Fred Waring Chorale, the Legend Singers, James Brown, Dance, Country Western and Rock groups frequented Kiel Opera House. And, yes The Rat Pack, Atom Ant and The Boss.

Great Blues and Jazz artists including Lionel Hampton, Duke Ellington, Louie Armstrong, Ella Fitzgerald and Count Basie entertained in Kiel. A young Grace Brumbry and a young Beverly Sills sang in concert in Kiel Opera House as did Johnny Cash, Buck Owens, and Minnie Pearl. High school bands and choirs performed in the Opera House. Thousands of students received diplomas on its stage.

Thousands of St. Louis dancers and members of bands, orchestras and choral groups performed in Kiel Opera House. Baby boomers remember mostly rock and jazz concerts; and sporting events, rodeos and circuses in the Auditorium, on the other side of the sliding sound proof wall.

APPENDIX C.
BUSINESS/MARKETING/FINANCING PLANS

Submitted by Ed Golterman and/or Kiel For Performing Arts, Inc.
1998-2007

Choices Grow Great Cities

This 32-page proposal was presented in July, 1998 to Urban Land Institute Panel, The mayor, The Comptroller, president of the Board of Aldermen, Danforth Foundation, Kiel Partners, Post-Dispatch, St. Louis Business Journal, Suburban Journals, RCGA.

Choices Grow Great Cities was strengthened and included Palm Capital Financing plan and presented to Mayor Harmon, Comptroller Green, Aldermanic President Slay September 25, 1998, and to Mark Sauer, Kiel Partners and Alderwoman Marit Clark.

January 14, 1999. Strengthened K-FPA proposal now includes Palm Capital Financing Plan, participation of John Kinnamon, Burn Brae Dinner Theater; Tom Klein, Windows on Washington; and strengthened by Bill Neal. This document was delivered to Kiel Partners, City Officials. Mark Sauer of Kiel Partners: *Not one molecule of substance which prompted Post-Dispatch editorial-shut up and put the money on the table.*

November 13, 1999. Golterman offered to pay $100 to present business plan to the Lauries or to their representatives.

January 2000. Business Plan with Glennon Co. is submitted to all those in control.

January 14, 2000 Financing Plan to all, including Mark Sauer.

February. The Plan was sent to the *Post-Dispatch asking* the Post to lead. Sauer said: nothing can happen until he sees a financial plan. He was sent a financing plan.(City Comptroller Darlene Green authorized $250 million in bonds for a replacement ballpark on the basis of an economic study paid for by the Cardinals. There were to be four *independent* studies on a replacement ballpark).

Proposals submitted by Golterman and/or Kiel for Performing Arts featured the use of historic tax credits-a desired financing method for restoration of historic buildings and naming/sponsorships. The naming of the theaters and sub spaces could bring in up to $90 million. Some of this money could also help renovate City Hall.

Additional proposals were sent to a succession of lease holders — Kiel Partners, Clark Enterprises, the Lauries, and Dave Checketts/Sports Capital Partners through 2007.

APPENDIX D.
PETITIONS DEMOGRAPHICS

In fall of 1999, Bill and Nancy Laurie of Columbia, Missouuri, who controlled the Opera House by lease, indicated they wanted a 'sense' of the community on the matter. 'We are open-minded'. So...

Petitions to Reopen Kiel Opera House

Memorial Day and July 4th 1999, were big *signature-gathering* days. As were Washington Avenue Festival, Opening of Chain of Rocks Bridge, Taste of Central West End, French Festival, Taste of Clayton, Muny, Strassenfest, Loft Tour, Mail-Ins and Millennium Eve.

4,750 names

30% St. Louis City

40% St. Louis County

10% Southern Illinois: Madison, St. Clair, Franklin counties and out-state

10% St. Charles, Jefferson counties and out-state Missouri

10% visitors from other states

Open it now, not next week	*How can I help?*
Didn't they re-open it?	*Put me on the list*
Is it still there?	*I remember seeing..*
I graduated at Kiel	*So did I...*
We need it open	*Where is it?*

Submitted to: Board of Aldermen (Lewis Reed, 6th Ward) with copies to Aldermanic President Francis Slay and Comptroller Darlene Green.

Copies were also sent to the *Post-Dispatch, St. Louis American, Suburban Journals, Riverfront Times,* County Supervisor Buzz Westfall; Bob Bedell, president of The St. Louis Convention and Visitors Commission; David Darnell, Downtown Partners. (Feel free to make copies and distribute to businesses, agencies and individuals interested in a revitalization of Downtown St. Louis, particularly through cultural and entertainment attractions.)

December 1999 this input from the community was submitted to Bill and Nancy Laurie, and Dick Thomas, Paige Sports Entertainment.

Signatures

City of St. Louis — All Zip Codes, St. Louis County, St. Charles, Jefferson City.

Affton	Florissant	St. Charles	Mineral Point
Arnold	Glendale	St. Peters	Perryville
Ballwin	Hazelwood	University City	Washington
Barnhart	Jennings	Wildwood	Springfield
Berkeley	Kirkwood	Webster Groves	Villa Ridge
Bowling Green	Ladue	Town and Country	Sullivan
Brentwood	Lake St. Louis	Valley Park	Bowling Green
Bourbon	Lemay	Wentzville	Salem
Bridgeton	Manchester	Kansas City	Eureka
Clayton	Maplewood	Cuba	Farmington
Chesterfield	Maryland Heights	Defiance	Festus
Columbia	Normandy	Kirkland	Glencoe
Creve Coeur	Oakville	Potosi	House Springs
Dellwood	O'Fallon	Londell	Sedalia
DeSoto	Olivette	Isabella	St. Genevieve
Des Peres	Overland	Dittmer	Ft. Leonard Wood
Dunhill	Richmond Heights	Gainsville	High Ridge
Fenton	Shrewsbury	Farmington	
Ferguson	St. Ann	Marshall	

Illinois

Alton	Columbia	Granite City	Peoria
Bethalto	Carbondale	Grafton	Red Bud
Belleville	Defiance	Greenville	Shamburg
Cahokia	Dorsey	Highland	St. Jacob
Centralia	East St. Louis	Jerseyville	Swansea
Champaign	Edwardsville	Madison	Teutopolis
Chester	Fairview Heights	Mascoutah	Troy
Collinsville	Freeburg	Millstadt	Valmeyer
Chicago	Glen Carbon	New Athens	Waynesville
Caseyville	Godfrey	O'Fallon	Waterloo
			Arlington Heights

ARKANSAS
Eureka Springs

IDAHO
Tadville

INDIANA
Indianapolis

KANSAS
Kansas City
Wichita

KENTUCKY
Lexington
Providence

MARYLAND
Towson
Cockeysville

MICHIGAN
Calloway
Cadillac

OKLAHOMA
Tulsa

TEXAS
Houston

TENNESSEE
Memphis
Nashville
Ripley
Woodburry
Clarksville

VIRGINIA
Vienna

WISCONSIN
Madison

WASHINGTON
Seabeck

Note: Summer of 2002, Ed Golterman *toured* an historic display of Kiel Opera House-original autographed photos, programs and ads as well as the plaque designated it a National Historic Place. Goal: present plaque to City in the fall along with 10,000 signatures on honor scroll. He has made repeated requests of those who control Kiel Opera House to put up the plaque. No response.

APPENDIX E.
CALLS FOR LEGAL ACTION

Printed in St. Louis Business Journal, August 17, 1998

On a day when thousands of residents of all persuasions in the St. Louis region, and many visitors from Chicago, enjoyed Strassenfest, the Rams and the Cardinals downtown, another nail has been driven into the coffin of our great civic opera house. The City will not (at least at this point) pursue legal action. Kiel Opera House always was a civic performance place for all groups, at reasonable rentals and with reasonable admission prices. It never was an exclusive facility in any way.

Mayor Clarence Harmon's lack of leadership and the City's lack of courage to address the issue on behalf of the people erodes regional trust in our core City. This puts a damper on other downtown projects.

Perhaps the people's interests and well-being might be best served by a courageous attorney. The attorney would file a lawsuit against those involved in the intentional, deep-damage to the opera house complex in 1994–1995, and the quiet commandeering of much of its space by the Kiel Center side. The suit would seek immediate return of space, repairs, restoration of a state-of-the art sound barrier, and putting in a new load-in area. The suit would also seek damages for lost jobs, wages, taxes, commerce, business, and tourism over the five years since the promised 1995 opening.

Penalties should also be sought for substantial delay of a cultural rebirth of downtown St. Louis, which is much needed. A partial guide for such a suit would be what the Chicago Opera House does for the Chicago economy.

With the physical evidence-irrefutable and the discovery phase narrow, such legal action should not take long. What this attorney really would be fighting for is more than dollars, but for a restoration of trust and honor.

The Author

"They sliced into it like with a meat cleaver"
Long-time City employee

The Honorable Janet Reno   October 6, 1999
Attorney General of the United States
The Justice Department
Washington, D.C.

Amid your myriad duties would you please review and share with our new U.S. Attorney, Eastern District of Missouri, this request to investigate and uncover the criminal activity in the destruction of the Kiel Auditorium in St. Louis, the damage and looting of Kiel Opera House and the eventual destruction of the St. Louis arena, achieved under the same lease agreement 1991-1992.

These buildings, which belong to the people of St. Louis, have been (are being sacrificed) to protect two greedy monopolies — the Fox Theater at midtown and Kiel Partners/Kiel Center, downtown. The multi-level crimes involve protecting or solidifying these monopolies, were and are directly engineered and caused by these entities.

Your investigation will show:

- Breaking lease agreements, other written commitments and publicized promising the Opera House would be renovated and reopened in 1994, along with opening of the new Kiel Center. That understanding was part of the basic deal, providing substantial tax breaks to developers of Kiel Center.

- The actual physical damage and theft of equipment, fixtures, furniture, artifacts and equipment from Kiel Auditorium and Kiel Opera House.

- Direct roles played by Fox Associates, Grand Center, Kiel Partners, their legal and public relations *agents,* board members, and others, in the nine-year conspiracy to destroy any and all competition-especially keeping Kiel Opera House closed.

- Involvement of the Smithsonian, as a possible tenant of a gutted or re-*configured* Kiel Opera House proposed by a St. Louis museum group. Officers of this group represent Grand Center and Fox Theater interests and/or have direct business dealings in and around Grand Center. One officer signed the lease of 1992, and is now trying to complete destruction of the Opera House. Another has real estate developments in and around Grand Center.

- Commissioning biased, slanted studies, paid for and dominated by Grand Center, the Fox Theater and Kiel Partners. (Consultants with ties to Grand Center and/or to a proposed performance arts center at The University of Missouri-St. Louis.)

- Possible payoffs and bribes of past and current city officials, and at least, a *perceived* threat by those who advance monopolies to withhold future help from a *nearly* helpless city, if they do not get their way. (City Officials bowing to wishes of monopolists).

- Collusion between Downtown Now and Grand Center to keep Kiel Opera House closed, despite overwhelming public support expressed at a dozen Downtown Now public meetings. The relationships between the Director of Downtown Now former President of Downtown St. Louis Partnership and Executive Director of Grand Center.

- Lies and misinformation on the condition of Kiel Opera House, its potential to help *spark* downtown revival and what other cities are doing.

- Silence of the St. Louis Post-Dispatch, which should have investigated this as early as 1992 and demanded indictments against the collaborators.

- The ultimate economic criminality is to leave downtown St. Louis culture-less relative to performing arts while dozens of other U.S. cities are using performing arts to spark downtown revitalization.

There is more than enough evidence in the public domain for the Justice Department to initiate an inquiry on behalf of the people of the St. Louis area, as opposed to a citizen or citizens filing suit. And, there is enough interstate involvement to make it federal.

I will be happy to share materials, documents, and information I have gathered over several years, tracking this criminality. Also, other citizens will come forth to assist your investigation.

The Author

Hon. Janet Reno   January 1, 2000
Attorney General of the United States
Justice Department
Washington, D.C.

Dear Attorney General Reno:

Would you kindly review and share with your newly-appointed U.S. Attorney — Eastern District of Missouri — the following information tracing the methodical destruction of cultural *treasures* belonging to the people of St. Louis to foster and perpetuate monopolies?

The destruction of Kiel Auditorium in downtown St. Louis, damaging and looting of Kiel Opera House, and destruction of The Arena — all owned by the people of St. Louis. This was achieved through a 1992 lease agreement between the City and Kiel Partners.

The continued assault on the Kiel Opera House, toward its final destruction (with the latest *option* involving the Smithsonian, is the unrelenting goal of the Fox Theater/Grand Center in midtown, and Kiel Center, downtown). Kiel is one of the world's finest music halls, and a six-venue civic center. Your investigation will show:

- Preferred bonding rates extended to Kiel Partners based on restoration and re-opening a civic center — Kiel Opera House. The Kiel Convention Hall was destroyed, not restored, the Opera House was neither restored nor re-opened. The bond rate was attained through fraud, anti-trust law violations, the breaking of written agreements and of publicized promises to re-open the Opera House in exchange for substantial tax breaks and City approval of the project.

    The same lease also called for severe no-compete stipulations that may even have precluded the Opera House' reopening.

- Physical damage including slicing off about 70 dressing rooms on the Opera House side, damaging or reducing the load-in capability, substantial damage to the stage surface, leaving the Opera House open to the elements for eighteen months, plus heavy encroachment into other Opera House *spaces*.

- Direct and indirect roles played by Fox Associates, Grand Center, Kiel Center, their officers, boards, legal, public relations and other representatives, and agents directly or indirectly involved in their intended destruction of these buildings. The roles of operators of other entertainment venues, not even in the City,

You will discover involvement of the Smithsonian as a –possible tenant for a *re-configured* Opera House. The Smithsonian has entered into an agreement to study using the Opera House as a depository for some of its stored items. The St. Louis group included Alan Bornstein, attorney with Sonnenschien, Nath and Rosenthal; Al Kerth III, a public relations executive, who signed the 1992 lease and who has been the *instrument* in misinforming and misleading the public on these matters; and developer Richard Baron.

They sent in an architect to design Kiel for re-use, which means-gutting it first. Steven Miller and Donna Laidlaw, Union Station Partners, were part of the group. USP kicked in $100,000 for the study, Clark Enterprises-$100,000 and Danforth Foundation-$100,000.

The author went to the Smithsonian in October 1999 and learned first hand they never wanted the Opera House. This was confirmed by Post-Dispatch Washington Correspondent Phil Dine. St. Louisans had been deceived for more than a year.

Your investigation will show the commissioning, slanting and funding of various studies aimed at preventing the Opera House from presenting music again. (to protect the Fox Theater).

Consultants of the Urban Land Institute and from the 2004 study were told in advance to find other uses. Several of these consultants had direct conflicts of interest through past or current consulting jobs for a proposed performance arts center at University of Missouri – St Louis, and for Grand Center entities.

Urban Land Institute Task Force

At least 26 members of the 42 member Task Force directly or indirectly represented Kiel Partners, Clark Enterprises, Grand Center and the Fox, or other theatrical entities or legal and financial suppliers to same. Some other members of the task force felt *intimidated* and *bullied*. This is a matter of public record, and can be confirmed. (*Riverfront Times*, D.J. Wilson). On the task force were:

David Fay, president of Fox Associates who stated he wanted the Opera House *gone.* The Grand Center point-man wants to destroy Kiel Opera House.

Attorney Steve Cousins, Armstrong Teasdale and/or Mrs. Cousins are officers of Grand Center and/or on boards of cultural and entertainment entities at midtown. Cousins or his law firm may do legal work for Grand Center entities.

Mark Sauer, president of The St. Louis Blues and Kiel Center who has said music would never be presented in Kiel Opera House again, that it was *a dog.*

Ann Ruwitch, president of Grand Center.

Traci Johnson, Mercantile Bank — Prime lender and financial institution for Grand Center entities and one of Kiel Partners.

Father Biondi and *Kathy Brady,* St. Louis University, aligned with Grand Center.

Mark Bernstein, Repertory Theater of Webster Groves. St. Louis.

Marit Clark, then-sixth Ward Alderwoman, who may do legal work for Grand Center. Practices in Clayton, Missouri.

Steve Engelhardt, city comptroller's office, campaigning to turn Kiel into a Blues/Jazz museum.

Comptroller Darlene Green, stonewalling logical uses, wants it turned into a Blues Jazz museum. She was not open to discussion or negotiations.

Dick Fleming, RCGA, will not tell St. Louisans how other cities use performing arts to revitalize downtowns.

Bob Bedell, St. Louis Convention and Visitors Commission. Administers large amounts of taxpayers money to bring tourists to St. Louis. His agency has taken Kiel Opera House off maps and promotional material. While theater tourism is helping revitalize downtowns. Bedell protects Grand Center. I have called for his resignation.

Wil Gregory, Downtown Partnership, committed to protecting Grand Center and the Fox, counter to its mission of revitalizing downtown.

Ron Himes, Black Rep. which is housed in Grand Center.

Al Kerth III, PR spokesperson for Civic Progress, Kiel Center during development, and one of the proponents of *let's turn it into a Smithsonian.* Mr. Kerth was quoted in 1992 in promising Kiel Opera House would be done first class. Formerly a Fleishman-Hillard Sr. VP., Mr. Kerth's new ventures were *seed funded* by John Danforth.

Dan Krasnoff, St. Louis Development Corp. Drafted the biased limited scope ULI briefing document that in effect instructed consultants to find *any other use but music* for the Opera House. There is a need to find out the influences and input of Mark Sauer and David Fay on his study, and if any *considerations* were rendered, to slant the study. The Fox and Kiel Partners basically paid for the study. They controlled the results. It was not an independent study.

Joanne LaSala, St. Louis 2004, (has since resigned). 2004 did their own biased study saying Kiel Opera House was not needed, everything should go into Grand Center. That study was summarily rejected in an open meeting in Grand Center.

Maureen McAvey, former head of St. Louis Development Corp. with ties with the ULI consultants, may have been some kind of cross-deals here-previous jobs/new jobs/and or assignments.

Mike McMillan, alderman for Grand Center's ward. Why is he on this task force?

Jill McGuire, Regional Arts Commission, is headquartered in Grand Center, RAC liberally funds Grand Center entities.

Steve Miller, Union Station Partners. One of the *Smithsonian* bunch.

Vallarie Patton, NationsBank. Another member of Kiel Partners

Wayman Smith, Anheuser-Busch, a Civic Progress company.

Steve Schankman, Contemporary Productions. Once offered to buy the Opera House.

Norman Seay, A fair man who listened to my side even though he is at UMSL, which is planning its own theater.

Chester Hines, Mayor's Office. This pattern of destruction started in the administration of Vince Schoemehl and was advanced during the term of Freeman Bosley. Mayors have not been protectors of the peoples' treasures. City officials have stated publicly that the City was afraid to sue because these people are our benefactors. Investigation will show that this was a stacked, unfair and biased study group. Briefing documents and reports by consultants will confirm that.

Urban Land Institute Task Force meetings were held in the afternoon on weekdays in a small conference room at Kiel Center. They were described as open to the public, but were very poorly publicized. Two ULI consultants had consulted on UMSL performing arts project and or Grand Center projects. *Conflicts of Interest.*

The Web

- Collusion between Downtown Partners (Downtown Now) and Grand Center/Fox in keeping the Opera House out of the revitalization of downtown "mix". The Former head of Downtown St.Louis/Downtown Partners,/Downtown Now is John Fox Arnold. His significant other is Ann Ruwitch, the Executive Director of Grand Center.

- At a series of Downtown Now public meetings, more than 50% of the tables reported out: Kiel Opera House Now after round table discussion. The Opera House was never put on the agenda for the next public meeting.

Recently, Thomas Reeves was appointed president of Downtown Partners. He is Chairman of Grand Center. Reeves cannot protect the Fox and revive downtown.

I asked him to tell the people of St. Louis where he stands, then, to resign because of conflict of interest. Controlling boards are all the same people.

Intimidation of a Municipal Government

In 1994 some City officials wanted to sue Kiel Partners to make them reopen Kiel Opera House. 28th Ward Alderman Dan McGuire led that fight in and out of the board of aldermen. City counselors said they didn't think the City had a good case. Privately and publicity City officials felt intimidated by Walter Metcalfe's threats that Civic Progress might withhold further support if the City pursued it.

- Some St. Louis city officials have said publicly they were afraid to sue Kiel Partners because these are the same people who are the City's benefactors in other matters. So, a city government is controlled by the money-providers. How can an intimidated city government make the city healthy again?

- You will find payoffs, contributions, bribes, and other influences on City officials by or on behalf of the Fox Theater, Grand Center, Kiel Partners and Civic Progress to keep Kiel Opera House closed. Some should be public record, others may be harder to find.

Kiel Center Lease—Restrictive, Damaging, Not Civic

- Possible direct and criminal conflict of interest on the part of Attorney Walter Metcalfe, Jr., a founder of Grand Center (St Louis Business Journal) drafting and signing the lease of '92 which destroyed the Kiel Convention Hall, damaged and looted Kiel Opera House and eventually destroyed the St. Louis Arena on a restrictive no-compete section of the lease. The clear economic retardation of downtown St. Louis by destroying Performing arts facilities while other cities refurbish and re-open more and more to spark revitalization.

Please consider that there is more than enough information in the public domain to begin an intensive investigation. There is also interstate commerce and use of postal service to advance these crimes. So, this is federal.

The most despicable on-going criminal activity is the continuous lying to the people of St. Louis and the withholding of accurate information, with no fear of being discovered or called to account.

The *St. Louis Post-Dispatch* has let the people down big time. For example, the president of Clark Enterprises (operators of Kiel Center) Mark Sauer is quoted in the P-D that the back stage of the Opera House is gone, or has been destroyed. If this is true then it is criminal destruction. It is not true. The Opera House retains one of the largest indoor stages in the world. The stage has actually gained space.

What was lost was an extension into the adjoining convention hall. You could open up the two halls by sliding open the massive soundproof walls. This was done occasionally. Saying the backstage is gone is a lie. The back stage is still there.

The Fox's president David Fay says the Opera House would cost taxpayers a lot of money. No. Private funding would be used. The project would create jobs, revenue income and contribute to a revitalized downtown. Tax revenues to the City will increase substantially.

Free from Fear, Many Would Come Forth

I believe many St. Louisans who live in fear of these controlling entities would come forward in any investigation. I have been tracking these matters for several years and will share all the information I have. Kiel Opera House is one of the finest in the world, the only large theater remaining in St. Louis that was built for large theatrical production and intimate concerts. Kiel was home of the St. Louis Symphony for 29 years and a preferred tour stop for the Metropolitan. It was always a civic facility with reasonable rentals and admission prices.

It drew entertainers from all types of musical disciplines — jazz, rock, blues, symphonic, individual artists; and audiences from seven surrounding states.

The Ambassador Theater downtown was torn down (1995) while other cities restore and re-open old theaters. The 10,000-seat Kiel Auditorium destroyed (1993–1994) the 3,500-seat Kiel Opera House and four smaller theater/auditoriums was closed and kept closed.

The Arena was destroyed in 1999, through the *no-compete* clause in Kiel Center lease.

These acts run counter to restoration efforts in other cities. There must be a very close look at the influences brought to bear on these City officials.

The people pay the *heaviest* price when sports *gods* rule-tax money, higher prices for events, limited choices. In the context of *threats to leave or enticements to draw,* sports franchises get what they want. Taxpayers and citizens usually pay a heavy burden. Within this context and under fear the Blues might leave St. Louis, Kiel Convention Hall was destroyed, Opera House damaged, and The Arena eventually destroyed to create Kiel Center and bring the Blues downtown. The City provided the official mechanisms.

The Lauries are getting Kiel Center, the Blues and the lease to Kiel Opera House (with re-development rights) for about $100 million. Laurie also took on debts.

The low price tendered by Kiel Partners/Clark Enterprises was to *keep the Blues in St. Louis* they had turned down double the offer. Can they sell a civic center? And, can the City, which still owns the Opera House give the Lauries re-development rights?

Two weeks ago, I filed a nomination of Kiel Opera House as one of 2000's Most-Endangered historic sites. I asked the National Trust for Historic Preservation to help the people of the St. Louis save what is left of our cultural resources.

The Honorable Jay Nixon   January 8, 2000
Attorney General – State of Missouri
Jefferson City, MO 65102

Dear Attorney General Nixon:

Would you consider coming to the aid of St. Louis area residents as consumers and tax payers by exposing and prosecuting as the law dictates those who have perpetrated the fraud:

a.) that the Smithsonian Institution was considering Kiel Opera House as a possible location for a satellite or branch (they were not)

b.) that the City of St. Louis is *holding out* a Smithsonian in the Gateway Mall area in seeking more tax money from City and County residents for infrastructure help. Please protect citizens, and taxpayers from a second possible fraud.

Please understand that the Smithsonian and other museum ideas for Kiel emerged through the ULI study as an attempt by the Fox, Grand Center and Kiel Partners to destroy Kiel as a music and performance venue.

The fraud — extended and communicated by the St. Louis *Post-Dispatch* is that the people of St. Louis would be so impressed with the name Smithsonian, they would not mind the gutting, destruction of, or crippling of the Opera House. That is not the case. People understand what the Opera House is and what it can contribute to downtown St. Louis and not as a museum.

I went to the Smithsonian in Washington D. C. on Friday October 8th, and heard directly from Michael Carrigan, Affiliations Deptartment, that the Smithsonian never wanted Kiel Opera House. *Post-Dispatch* National Correspondent Phil Dine confirmed this in The Post on Saturday, October 9th. It is sad when a private citizen has to expose fraud perpetrated on the people.

The *Post-Dispatch* didn't use its power to clarify that the Smithsonian did not find the Opera House, a great music and special events building, appropriate for a museum. They let the impression *lay out there before the people.* This is not journalistic responsibility.

Your investigators will find that the officers of something called the St. Louis Museum Corporation affiliated with the Smithsonian have business or other ties to Grand Center and the Fox. One of the proponents, Al Kerth III, also signed the 1992 lease that destroyed the Kiel Convention Hall, damaged and looted the Opera House and finally destroyed the Arena on *no-compete.*

Please protect our citizens from further fraud. Demand that St. Louis produce a letter of commitment from the Smithsonian before the Downtown Now plan can hold that *carrot* out before state legislators or voters.

In St. Louis we have a history of valuable cultural buildings being destroyed *on the come* because something might happen. I will be happy to assist you in your investigation.

The Hon. Marvin Price, Jr.   June 15, 2000
Chief, Antitrust Div./Justice Department
209 S LaSalle S600, Chicago, IL. 60604

The Hon. Audrey G. Fleissig
United States Attorney, Eastern Missouri
1114 Market Street S401, St. Louis, MO 63192

Would you investigate violations of anti-trust laws, conflicts of interest, and physical damage to civic property, relative to the destruction of Kiel Auditorium, the damaging and looting of Kiel Opera House and the destruction of the Arena–all generated through the same lease document of 1992?

Would you focus your investigations on the controlling or influencing roles of Grand Center, the Fox Theater and Kiel Partners-primary conspirators in keeping Kiel Opera House closed?

Would you investigate three biased studies aimed at destroying Kiel Opera House and influences of Grand Center, the Fox, and Kiel Partners on these studies? These studies were undertaken between 1997 and 2000.

Would you investigate the theft of items from Kiel Opera House and Auditorium and make attempts to recover them? They belong to the people of St. Louis.

Would you please investigate the perpetuation of these anti-trust violations by an entity called Paige Sports Entertainment, new lease-holders of Kiel Center?

Would you investigate unauthorized use of the Smithsonian as a possible re-use tenant, toward destroying the main theater? (Please refer to my correspondence of January 11 and May 2 for background). I am sure many St. Louisans would come forward and assist in helping a redress of these grievances. Would you indicate by note or e-mail, your selected course or courses of action?

Regards,

The Author

cc: Missouri Attorney General Jay Nixon

For Immediate Release June 19, 2000
Kiel Opera House misses *Eleven Most Endangered* List
Will Re-Submit for 2001

Kiel Opera House missed this year's list of America's Eleven Most-
Endangered Historic Places, but St. Louisan Ed Golterman will re-nom-
inate the Opera House for the 2001 listing by the National Trust for
Historic Preservation.

*In the '90s, we lost The Convention Hall, The Arena, The Ambassador Building
and Ambassador Theater. The Opera House was damaged, remains closed, and under
attack,* said the grandson of one of Kiel's founders.

Of course, I'm going to re-submit. Time is an enemy. Golterman received
a letter today from the National Trust's David Brown, stating the Opera
House would not be one of the Eleven Most-Endangered, announced on
June 26th. I will re-submit the Opera House for consideration for placement
on the 2001 list.

The Author

The Hon. Jay Nixon, Missouri Attorney General December 21, 2001
The Hon. Jennifer Joyce, St. Louis Circuit Attorney
The Hon. Ray Gruender, U.S. Attorney. Eastern Missouri
Missouri State Auditor Laura McCaskill
Anti Trust Chief Price, Justice Department

As Grand Center and sports franchise owners waste Kiel Opera House a
sixth year, I again call for investigations into violations of civil and criminal
laws against the people and their property. And, seek redress for the peoples'
losses:

- Deliberate damage, looting and neglect of Kiel Opera House in
  downtown St. Louis to render it inoperable for large-scale theatrical production: physical evidence.

- Frauds dating back to the original Kiel Partners deal-publicized
  and contractual responsibility to reopen the Opera House as part
  of a great civic, entertainment and sports center. Participants,

documents, procedures creating and/or concealing *escape-clause* documents, allowing Kiel Partners and their successor leaseholders to not reopen the Opera House.

- Payoffs to candidates and office holders over at least four City administrations, and/or intimidation of same — *The carrot and the stick.*

- Unethical conduct on the part of attorneys, primarily (but not limited to) principals of Bryan Cave, One Met Square, on behalf of so-called downtown promoters and tourism promoters, and Grand Center.

- Conflicts of interest, anti-trust law violations.

- Depriving the people of St. Louis of jobs, income, benefits, and the City of tax revenue.

- Application of public money on collaborations to waste and/or gut the main theater of Kiel Opera House, including fraudulent studies with pre-determined outcomes.

- Political contributions of between $500,000–$1 million to keep Kiel Opera House closed or to get rid of it altogether (enclosed)

The Author

Ed GOLTERMAN — Producer
614 Wooddell Court
Saint Louis MO 63122
12/07/05

Mr. James Crowe, Junior
U.S. Attorney's Office Eastern District of Missouri
Eagleton Federal Building
111 S. 10th Street
St. Louis MO 63102

Dear Jim:

In a week or so I will forward the updated Saving Kiel. In the meantime, there is another valid point-of-entry into stopping the continued restraint of trade of Kiel Opera House and Muny. The influence and money spent by the Danforth Foundation and the Fox Foundation in these pursuits violates anti-trust law.

The Danforth Foundation spent millions and assembled and assigned other millions to kill Kiel Opera House from 1997 through at least 2003, and perhaps continues to do so. The Fox Foundation paid off the Muny Board in August of 2003 to limit their 2004 season.

These are valid entry points, along with physical damage to Kiel Opera House, conflicts of interests of a flock of attorneys, the same attorneys with the same clandestine objectives sitting on all sides of the table, and massive payoffs to City officials going back at least to Schoemehl. And of course, the central roles of the owners of the Fox Theater and Grand Center.

Please let me know what else I can provide. The urgency of course is that said restraint-of-trade has rendered St. Louis a non-destination. This has severely reduced our convention, group travel and travel-for-entertainment business.

We cannot compete against cities and towns with downtown performing arts centers. The annual loss is $350 million a year. Renaissance Grand is about to go under and Union Station will be next. The enclosed shows you the competitive disadvantage St. Louis is forced to operate under and why we are no longer competitive.

Ed Golterman

314 909-724   fax 314 966-6649   edkielo@gtw.net

CALLS FOR LEGAL ACTION

March 6, 2006
The Hon. Catherine Hanaway
cc: J. Crowe, M. Reap

Dear Catherine:

Right now Kiel Opera House is being *sold out* again — by another mayor, the fourth, by another lease holder, the fourth, to *protect* the Fox Theater. This is criminal. All the previous *sell outs* were criminal. *Open up* The Savvis deal right now. Stop Grand Center right now.

Ed Golterman
ED GOLTERMAN
614 Wooddell Court
Saint Louis, MO 63122

January 27, 2007

The Hon. Catherine Hanaway
U.S. Attorney, E. District-MO

The Hon. Michael Reap
Assistant U.S. Attorney

The Hon. James E Crowe, Jr.
Criminal Div. U.S. Attorney

Thomas Eagleton Court House
111 S 10th 20th Floor
Saint Louis, MO 63102

The *mugging* of Kiel Opera House and squeezing Muny to less than seven weeks a year to *Protect* the Fox Theater are Civic Progress' greatest crimes. These text-book violations of anti-trust laws have proven most harmful to St Louis' ability to compete for conventions, group travel and travel-for-entertainment business. They *signaled* Civic Progress' taking control over St. Louis municipal government. And, they are barbaric.

Through its banks, lawyers, lobbyists, money, pressure, control of civic and cultural *boards*, and protected by its media 'shills', Civic Progress is *TIF-raping* the City, trying to take over the school board again, raiding the MOHELA student loan fund to build Danforth's research labs and *raping* Forest Park. It clearly demonstrates its continued control over governments and disenfranchises the voter.

Your agency has been derelict to have not prevented these crimes in their planning stages, prior to their execution, and continues to be negligent in not indicting those who ordered these crimes to be carried out by their *agents* in the business community, lobbyists, government officials and their *shills* in the media.

You have had in your possession for many years more than enough *discovery* and *reasonable cause* to have taken action, preventing St. Louis from being rendered the most corrupt, inept, failed, and controlled city in America. You and your predecessors have chosen to not act.

Accompanying this letter is a copy of the updates of information I have provided you in summary, each year since 1998. You have information from other sources and from the public domain. You can read the newspapers. Better late than never? May be. It is getting rather late. Indict and prosecute them ALL.

Ed L. Golterman

Cc: without attachment: Mowbray-PD Sherberg-Business Journal Finkel RFT, News Directors-St. Louis Radio and Television Stations.

314 909-7224   fax 314 966-6649   edkielo@gtw.net

APPENDIX F.
KIEL FOR PERFORMING ARTS - TEAM
(September 1998 – January 1, 2000)

Board Members Professional Services
Volunteer, Paid or In Kind

Gary Bill, Publisher, Developer
Charlene Bry, Publisher
Joan Caro, Performer
H. Russell Carter, Historian
Peggy Eggers, Midwest Lyric Opera
Joseph Dubuque, Investment Broker
Jennifer Grotpeter, St. Louis Resident
Ed Golterman, Chairman
James Heidenry, Developer
Michael Henderson, Security Firm
Gary C. Hoffman,
    Tarlton Construction Co.
Alan Steinberg, Attorney
Jarred Baccus, Composer
Suzanne Hunn, Realtor
St. Louis Board of Aldermen,
    Resolution
4700 Signers of Petitions to Reopen
900 Plus Letters, Faxes and E-mails
Taki Sugitani, Violinist
Post-Dispatch, Editorials
Suburban Journals, Editorial
St. Louis Jewish Light, Feature
St. Louis Times, Feature
Paul Westlake, Jr. Architect, Cleveland
Dan Jackson, Developer
200 and contributors
Marilyn S. Wingbermuehl,
    St. Louis Ballet

Gwen Buss, Plaza Square Apartments
Willie Obermoehler, A-V Technican
Evan Schwartzfarb, Palm Capital
Ron O'Connor, Public Relations
Susan Roach, Attorney
Peter van Dijk, Architect, Cleveland
John Kinnamon, Burn Brae Theater
Sam Glaser, Developer
Tom Klein, Windows on Washington
Regional Arts Commission
Rallo Contracting
Burt Holtzman, Patron of the Arts
Elliot Liebson, Public Policy
Monica McFee, Public Relations
Bill Neal, SLDC
Chau-Giang Nguyen, Pianist
Mark Philips, Developer
Elle Stewart, Windsor Theater Group
Jeff Stewart, Windsor Theater Group
Rev. Mike Tooley Centenary United
Peter Vaccaro, Performer
Mallarie Zimmer- Intermission Magazine
Kevin McCameron, Intermission
    Magazine
Glennon Company, Marketing Firm
Joe Ragni, Radio Sales Executive
St. Louis Core Newspaper
Teresa Daniels Dance Studio
Diane Rosen, Interior Designer

APPENDIX G.
THE POWER CORRIDOR

If you painted a swatch five blocks wide up the middle of St. Louis from Broadway to Forest Park you would highlight the St. Louis *power* corridor—banks, law firms, foundations, cultural and entertainment entities, PR firms, newspaper and radio and TV stations who *work* Civic Progress' will over City Hall and the people of St. Louis.

One Metropolitan Square at 200 N. Broadway houses the Danforth Foundation, the Gateway Foundation, Jack Danforth's law firm Bryan Cave, the Regional Chamber and Growth Association, St. Louis Sports Commission, and until a year ago, the St. Louis Convention and Visitors Commission.

If Civic Progress *shapes* its deals in the quiet of a country club board room, they take shape and *roll out* from One Met Square. Fleishman Hillard Public Relations Firm, 200 North Broadway, *sells* the deals

One Memorial Drive contains KMOX Radio and KMOV TV. Moving West on Market, Pine, Olive or Locust are the banks — UMB, Bank of America, KSDK-TV, General America Life, Laclede Gas, AT&T.

The Post-Dispatch is at 900 N. Tucker, just a bit north of the power corridor. Civic Progress companies pour millions in advertising dollars into the Post. Its current publisher, Kevin Mowbray, is a member of Civic Progress as is the current General Manager of KMOX radio.

City Hall, pretty much controlled by Civic Progress, is at Tucker and Market. At 14th and Market is the closed Kiel Opera House, the 'dead' Memorial Plaza, and Aloe Plaza. Behind the Opera House is Scottrade Center, the thrice-named home of the St. Louis Blues. At Jefferson and Market are the offices of the Metropolitan Sewer District and Wachovia, who bought A. G. Edwards early in 2007.

Two miles west, we come to Grand Center—the seat of cultural and entertainment power: Fox Theater, Powell Hall, Grandel Theater, Sheldon Concert Hall, Contemporary Art Museum, Arts and Education Council and St. Louis University.

A block west of Grand on Olive is public television station KETC—a blatant commercial outlet for the Fox and other Grand Center entities.

Three miles west is the Central West End, where many of the *movers and shakers* live. Forest Park is just west of Kings highway between Lindell and Clayton, re-shaped to Civic Progress' image. The tax-supported Zoo, museums and Science Center have become private party and event *places* and big-tax-write-offs depositories. Forest Park Forever is Civic Progress' control mechanism in The Park, limiting the Muny—the greatest outdoor theater in America—to seven weeks a summer and promoting a $150-million expansion of The Art Museum.

This power corridor—One Met Square to Forest Park, and its control over City Hall has nearly turned St. Louis into a *non-destination*.

APPENDIX H.
FOUNDATIONS

The author and/or Kiel For Performing Arts made repeated requests for foundations to assist in restoring and reopening the Opera House. In other cities this is what Foundations do. The following shows the reach and power of Civic Progress. Projects without their *blessing* receive neither corporate nor foundations support.

1998–1999

Anheuser-Busch Foundation	No	Civic Progress/Kiel Partners
Arts and Education Council	No	Don't Qualify
Enterprise Rent-A-Car Foundation	No	Andy Taylor is Chairman, Civic Progress
Danforth Foundation	No	They are funding studies to gut the Opera House. *Not approved on Downtown Now plan*
E. Desmond Lee Foundation	No	Supporting UMSL Performance Center
Junior League	No	Just, No.
Mercantile Foundation Center	No	Civic Progress/Kiel Partners/Grand
Metropolis Request for Project	No	Under control of 2004 Downtown Now
Missouri Arts Council	No	No reason
Monsanto Fund	No	Civic Progress/Kiel Partners
Regional Arts Commission	Yes	$5,000
Southwestern Bell Foundation	No	Civic Progress/Kiel Partners
St. Louis 2004	No	John Danforth, Joanne LaSalla
St. Louis Squires and Ladies	No	Present next year
Whitaker Foundation	No	Al Kerth III is on Board

Fox Charitable Foundation tightens nooses around Kiel and Muny

Foundations control by what they decide to fund and what they decide to not fund.

APPENDIX I.
USE OF TAXPAYERS' MONEY

Planning is indeed a process of municipal government. However, study processes in St. Louis are taken to extreme. Too much of the taxpayers' money funds studies:

The Honorable Margaret Kelley   July 14, 2000
Auditor–State of Missouri Capitol Room 224
Jefferson City, MO 65101

Dear Auditor Kelley:

In late 1977, 1998, 1999, a series of attacks were mounted against Kiel Opera House by those who want to destroy it. Well over a million dollars was spent on three formal studies with this direct goal.

Undertaken about the same time, they had overlapping goals of crippling or gutting the main theater so it could not compete with the Fox or Kiel Center.

As auditor, perhaps you cannot address the funding of these studies by Kiel Partners, Danforth Foundation, St. Louis Union Station Partners and St. Louis 2004 and other private entities. However, the taxpayers of Missouri and St. Louis paid for a great deal of this effort aimed at destroying a civic, cultural and economic treasure that they own. (Kiel Opera House is still a municipal resource. Would you please investigate the misuse of public funds in salaries, benefits and administrative costs/expenses, primarily of the offices of the Comptroller and of the St. Louis Development Corporation (but not exclusive to these departments?) This use of City employees and related expenditures bunched up before, during and after the studies undertaken to gut Kiel Opera House. The time frames here are late 1997 to mid 2000:

1. Maureen McAvey, Director; Dan Krasnoff, Planner, and staff of St. Louis Development Corp. Comptroller Darlene Green, her assistant, Steve Englehardt, both members of ULI Task Force and others in the Comptroller's office.

2. St. Louis 2004 Cultural Study — January 1998–December 1998- basically the same City officials, staff and support involved. Participation of St. Louis City officials and employees-to whatever degree.

3. Smithsonian Satellite. Participation of City employees, officials in study roughly from last quarter, 1998 through end of 1999, ostensibly to bring Smithsonian into a gutted theater. This was a fraud perpetrated on the people of St. Louis all along. The Smithsonian never wanted the Opera House. Also related, were City officials and employees working on the so-called Downtown Now Plan.

Despite public urging and the clear use of theater in other cities to help revitalize downtowns, the Downtown Now Plan refused to include the Kiel Opera House.

In St. Louis, it's the same people making the decisions, and they coordinate. When the *museums* plans did not fly, the options were handed off to Downtown Now. For several months the people of St. Louis were still told Kiel Opera House was slated for gutting and conversion into a museum.

Again, determine expenses of City employees, perhaps the same ones as involved in the other studies.

My guess is that pro-rated payroll information, expense reports, and the time allotted through assignments could be uncovered. Also, perhaps some outside resources — printers, binders, graphics, coordinated by the City, could be tracked. Too much money is spent in St. Louis destroying civic, cultural and economic resources.

This is a city that desperately needs to use its existing resources. The Ambassador Theater, the Kiel Convention Hall, the Arena, the damage and looting of the Opera House, all to protect monopolies.

The citizens, unprotected by government officials and to some extent, the media, vigorously opposed the findings of these studies and the processes. The Opera House is still here. Most of their proceedings were flawed, there were massive conflicts of interest and their rejection by the people were *logged* in the newspapers.

To the extent that you feel this could constitute misuse of public money, please consider looking into it and putting an end to such destructive practices. The issue is not whether or not the Opera House will ever come back. The issue is use of public funds to continue to try to destroy it.

The Author

July 20, 2000 — Same message to expanded list

The Hon. Claire McCaskill, Missouri Auditor;
Marvin Price, Jr., Chief Anti-Trust-Justice
Audrey Fleissig, US Attorney, Eastern Missouri.
Jay Nixon Attorney General, Missouri

October 2, 2000

The Honorable Claire C. McCaskill
State Auditor, Missouri, State Capitol
Jefferson City, Missouri 65101

Could your office look into the spending of taxpayers' money — City of St. Louis, St. Louis County and The State of MO in coordinated efforts to destroy Kiel Opera House.

This spending includes the salaries, benefits and time of paid city employees of several departments participating and coordinating at least three studies aimed at destroying the main theater. These studies were undertaken in 1997 and may continue today under new 'labels'. When they have been exposed to the public, the public has vigorously rejected their intent, their processes and their recommendations.

Primary agencies or departments involved are the St. Louis Development Corporation and the Comptroller's office (but not limited to these). Would you also look into or ask the Attorney General to look into the City's involvement in allowing the Lauries to sell the name Kiel off Kiel Center and keep the $70 million to pay private debt including hockey players' salaries? Kiel Center was proposed and communicated as a civic center and may still be defined as a civic center. A private entity should be given no opportunity to re-name or benefit financially from re-naming such a Center. City officials who allow this break trust with the people, and possibly the law.

Would you consider now stepping in and protecting what's left of the people's civic resources, when they are not protected by local officials or by the media?

The Author

Appendix J.
Companies Leaving/Loss of Corporate Headquarters

A 1% earnings tax on those who work in the City is at least partially blamed for companies and employees moving out. St. Louis needs income, badly, but is this a regressive tax relative to keeping companies or attracting companies. The flight of companies/loss of corporate headquarters is not just in the City.

TWA sold to American
Ralston Purina sold to Nestle
Celox Networks moves from the City to Westport Plaza
Mallinckrodt is sold to Tosco
Ernst and Young moves to Clayton
Husch and Eppenberger moves to Clayton
Eveready Batteries moves to Chesterfield
Southwestern Bell moves to Texas
McDonnell Douglas is sold to Boeing
Boatman's Bank is sold to Bank of America
Mercantile Bank is sold to Firstar
Monsanto is sold. Division remains in Olivette
Pet moved out
Wetterau is sold
Sherwood Medical moved out
Edison Brothers is sold
Ventures Stores Loss of Corporate Headquarters and Company
Missouri Pacific RR Loss of Corporate Headquarters and Company
St. Louis-San Francisco RR. Loss of Corporate Headquarters and Company
KTY Railroad Loss of Corporate Headquarters and Company
Cablofil moves to Mascoutah, Illinois
Hill-Behan Lumber Company closes

Bridge Information System declares bankruptcy
Aurora Foods leaves Union Station for Westport Plaza.
Purina Mills is sold to Land O' Lakes
Earthgrains is bought by Sara Lee
Dillard's closes in St. Louis Centre and Crestwood Plaza
Owners of the Adams Mark sell six hotels including its downtown property
Ralston Purina is purchased by Nestle
American Airlines de-hubs its Lambert Airport operation
May Department Stores is sold to Federated
Pulitzer Publishing is sold to Lee Enterprises

APPENDIX K.
PLAQUE HONORING KIEL OPERA HOUSE
AS NATIONAL HISTORIC PLACE

Built 1932-'33 — Opened 1934 — Closed 1991

You buy it, we'll put it up
–The City

We did. You didn't
–The author

January 8, 2002–Contributors

Advertising Club of Greater St. Louis
Angelique's Parlor
Associated General Contractors of St. Louis
Dr. Amy M. Bartels
John and Lori Campisi
Cherokee-Lemp Historic District
Michael G. and Jane Concannon
German American Heritage Society St. Louis
Golterman Historic Enterprises
The 'Hill' Business Association
Il Pensiero
Rick and Rita LaMonica
Lindbergh High School Band Flea Market
Mail Boxes Etc. Kirkwood, MO.
Misericordia Society
Metropolitan St. Patrick's Day Parade and Run in St. Louis

Jeannette Mott Oxford
New Jefferson Arms
2001 Parkway West Band Arts and Crafts Fair
St. Louis Times FUNFEST 2001–2002
St. Raymond's Church and The Cedars, Francis R. Slay
Sicilian Cultural Association of St. Louis
Alan and Joyce Steinberg
2001 Tilles Park Arts and Crafts Fair
Anthony and Lisa Troglio
UNICO- St. Louis Chapter
Peter Vaccaro Insurance
Windsor Theater Group Jeff and Ele Stewart
William J. Winter, Sr. Family

A project of:
Golterman Historic Enterprises

APPENDIX L.
TOUR OF KIEL EXHIBIT AND SIGNATURES

Honor It. Install Plaque. Re-Open It
(Late 2001 to October 2002)

Advertising Club Board and Officers	38
Alexandra School of Dance 9/20/02	50
All Cultures Festival Jefferson City 10/5/02	40
An Art Affair Westport Plaza	14
Art Dimensions 1/5/02	24
Belleville Art on the Square	460
Ballwin Days	35
Bastille Day, Soulard	150
Bevo Days 8/24/02	137
Blue Bird Park	17
Brentwood Days 9/20 21	62
Briscuso Dance Studio Ballwin	34
Charmette School of Dance 9/25/02	63
Cherokee-Lemp Neighborhoods	18
Columbus Day, The Hill 10/6/02	58
Eckert's Orchards	19
Farmers Market	76
Festival of Art Queeny Park 8/30–9/1 '02	157
Flea Market -Lindbergh High School Band	26
Florissant Old Towne Festival 10/13/02	103
Jefferson Arms	17
Jefferson Barracks Blast 7/3/02	14
Kimmswick Festival	24

Kirkwood Farmers Market 10/20/02	14
Kirkwood Green Tree Festival 9/13-15/02	119
Lindbergh Band Flea Market 9/8/02	25
Manchester Homecoming 9/6–8/02	88
Meramec Community Fair, Sullivan, MO	10
Missouri State Fair (Centennial) Sedalia, MO	920
Muny Forest Park	184
O' Fallon MO. Festival 10/12/02	101
Quincy Riverfest 9/15/02	73
St. Charles Riverfest	208
Springfield, Il Route 66 Festival 9/28/02	86
St. Louis Public Library	17
St. Louis Times Funfests	138
Shrine of St. Joseph Festival	65
Sunset Hills	67
Theresa Daniels Dance Studio 9/8/02	100
Tilles Park Arts and Crafts	111
Town and Country Fire and Ice	113
Webster Groves Public Library	6
Wentzville Crossings Keepsakes Show	107
West County Greek Festival	190
121 pages.	3,403
Previous	4,650
Letters, E-mails, Faxes	900
Total	9,953

ST. LOUIS SYMPHONY ORCHESTRA
VLADIMIR GOLSCHMANN, Conductor
1947 - 1948
SIXTY-EIGHTH SEASON

Printed in the United States
204379BV00001B/172-210/P